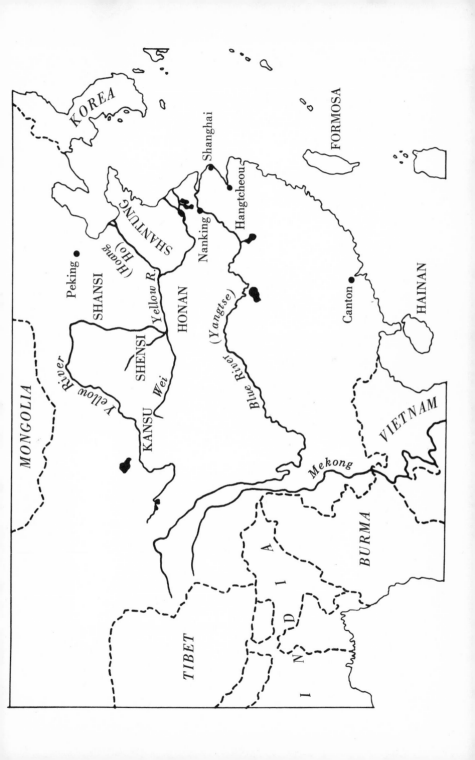

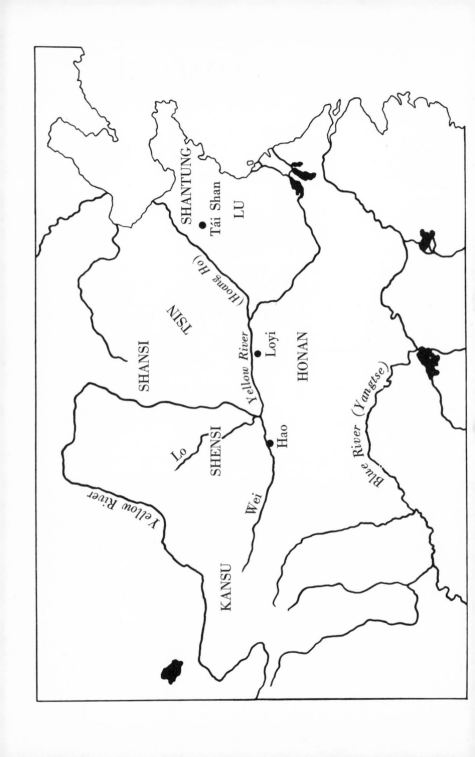

CONFUCIUS
and Chinese Humanism

CONFUCIUS
and Chinese Humanism

BY PIERRE DO-DINH

Translated by Charles Lam Markmann

FUNK & WAGNALLS ■ NEW YORK

To Jean Schlumberger,
whose example and friendship
have sustained me.
P. D.

孔子

與中國的人道主義

CONTENTS

CONFUCIUS
and Chinese Humanism

THE SOURCES

■ The fundamental source on Confucius is in a rather disorganized work called the *Luen yu,* frequently known as the *Conversations,* a collection of pupils' very terse notes on the Master's discussions with his disciples. Assembled rather belatedly, at least a century after the Master's death, it was cast in the form in which we know it under the Hans and the Sungs —in other words, many centuries later. Nonetheless, the work gives a certain impression of authenticity, apart from a few details. Confucius is shown to be a man and not a god. His teachings were also quoted and discussed in three other works written by or attributed to relatively far-removed disciples, including his grandson, K'ong Ki, and Mencius. These works are the *Ta Hio* (*The Great Study*), the *Chong Yong* (*The Golden Mean* or *The Invariable Mean*), and *Meng-tse* (*Mencius*). Together with the *Luen yu* they comprise the *shu*—"four books" or "four classics." To these must be added other classics, *king*, in theory antecedent to Confucius. They include a handbook of divination, *Y king* (*The Mutations*), which is cloaked in exaggerated mystery; a collection of songs and hymns, *She king* (*The Odes*); a collection of historical writings, *Shu king* (*The Documents*); a history of Lu, the country where Confucius was born; *Ch'uen Ts'yu* (*Spring and Autumn*); and a rather late book of ritual, *Li Ki* (*Notes on Rites*). This last was to be supplemented by two other books of ritual, *Chu Li* and *Yi Li*. The teachings of Confucius consisted in the faithful transmittal of this cultural inheritance, meditation on it, and veneration of it. Thus he founded a humanism and set limits to it. All these works, whether earlier or later than Confucius, are slender: *The Great Study* amounts to a single sentence and a small number of quotations, yet an amazing amount of wisdom was compressed into it.

1

The words and deeds of the Master of Lu are also to be found in commentaries, *chuan,* on the chronicle of *Spring and Autumn,* done independently of one another by three little-known figures, Tso, Ku-leang, and Kong-yang, and also in a very late work attributed to Wang Su (d. A.D. 256), *K'ong-tse Kia-yu (Sayings of the School of Confucius),* sometimes referred to simply as *Kia-yu,* which, however, might have been compiled from ancient traditions. And it is important not to omit the first biography of Confucius, the author of which was the great historian Sseu-ma Ts'ien. The biography appears in Chapter 47 of his *She ki (Historical Memoirs).*

Two of these works are referred to hereafter by abbreviations: *Luen yu* is *L. Y.* and *Chong Yong* is *Ch. Y.*

THE CHINESE AND THE BARBARIANS

■ The present geographical configuration of China dates from the end of the third century B.C., when the empire was established. It has no relation to the expanse of the original Chinese territory, which has been theoretically reconstituted in researches going back from this date to the dawn of the historical period.

The original territory lay in two plains of the Yellow River: in the east the alluvial Great Plain, which extended from Peking to the Huai and from the foothills of Shansi to the mountainous spur of Shantung, 620 miles long and wide at its maximum and enclosing some 125,000 square miles (somewhat more than England and Ireland combined); and a western plain embracing some 100,000 square miles in the basin of the Wei and the Lo. The low plain in the east was half under water; the plateaux in the west were covered with loess, the fertile crumbly yellow soil carried there by geological storms that whipped it out of

2

POLYCHROMATIC **EARTHEN JAR**
(NEOLITHIC PERIOD)

central Asia during the middle Paleolithic period. The east is
a land of rice, the west is a land of grain, and wheat grows
everywhere.

Communication between these two plains was via a narrow
corridor approximately 150 miles long through which the Yellow
River ran. Honan was the country that lay between, hence its
importance in the development of China: since the Neolithic
period, it seems to have been at the center of an international
trade route. This road led to the Ukraine in the west and to the
islands of the Pacific and Indian Oceans in the east, in communication with the civilizations of the Indus and the Nile and with
pre-Columbian America. Thus, we find in the Neolithic sites in
the west a polychromatic pottery that has been linked with the
art of Susa, Crete, and the Crimea, and in the east an industry
of which the tripod was characteristic. On the coast, between
Shantung and the bay of Hangchu, we find the so-called "black-
pottery civilization." Central China, the "Middle Kingdom,"

4

TRIPOD-BASED EARTHEN JAR
(NEOLITHIC PERIOD)

arose where these two currents moving in opposite directions intersected.

The Chinese were far from occupying the whole of this original domain. On the contrary, they were like an island surrounded by a "sea of the barbarians." The Tis were predominant in Shansi and the extreme north. The Jongs were everywhere, in Shensi, south of the Yellow River, on the seacoast, and in the Huai valley. The Yis lived in the eastern mountains of Shantung. The Tis were Altaic, Tunguz, or Tartar, in other words, the ancestors of the Turks (the word "turk," meaning "strong," dates only from the seventh century), the Mongols, and the Manchus. The Jongs, who perhaps were the real indigenous people, are identified by R. A. D. Forrest with the modern Miaos, and the same author links them linguistically with the Mon-Khmer group, whose representatives are scattered through Indochina, the Pegu district of Burma, Assam, and India (Cambodians, Mons, Khasis, Mundas, etc.).

5

There is nothing improbable in this belief. It corresponds to the slow infiltration by the peoples of northern Asia (in northern Siberia, in the region of the Yenessei, there is a small population whose language is Tibetan-Burmese) in a southerly direction. A rather indefinite Miao tradition traces that group's descent from Siberia, the land of polar days and nights. Southern China, inhabited by the Mans was not yet part of Chinese territory. A glance at a linguistic map will show that the Miaos, driven out of Honan in a southerly direction, are to the north of the Thais, hence, it is legitimate to suppose that the Mans were Thais. Their most important representatives are in Thailand, Burma, Assam, and the mountain region of North Vietnam. Their great wave dates only from the thirteenth century. They had entered Thailand from Yunnan, routed by the great Mongol campaign of Jenghiz Khan. And, until the third century, the old manuscripts speak of "little black men" in southern China—most certainly Negritos like those in the Philippines today. The Negrito and Australoid source has been confirmed for the whole of southeast Asia. The languages of Wu (in the Shanghai region) and Ch'u (in the basin of the Yangtse River) may have been polysyllabic and connected with Malay. Other linguistic arguments, which link Chinese and Tibetan, would argue for their origin in the region where the eastern borders of Tibet and the western borders of China meet. Perhaps the Sino-Tibetans represented the last wave of a Sinitic group comparable to the Indo-European whose members were the Chinese, the Tibetans, the Mons, the Khmers, the Thais, the Vietnamese, the Mundas, etc.—in short, virtually all the populations of eastern and southern Asia. The fact that the Chinese—scattered as they were in minuscule islets of population—regarded themselves nevertheless as Chinese suggests that they were not indigenous. That does not necessarily make them Indo-Europeans, as Conrady and later Terrien de la Couperie believed, in spite of the large number of Chinese words of Indo-European origin.* Maspéro, relying on the study of Chinese domestic ar-

---

* For example: *ma*, horse, which resembles the archaic High German

6

chitecture, has rejected this somewhat audacious theory. But the civilization proves nothing more as to its origins.

The barbarians were not only on the periphery of Chinese territory: they were everywhere, even around the capital of Loyang, living in the swamps and forests. Between the eighth and the sixth centuries B.C. there was not a single year in which there was no record of one of their raids on the citadels of central China. Proof of their power may be found in the fact that sometimes they contracted alliances by marriage with Chinese princely houses.

As has undoubtedly been the case of all other countries, China did not develop in isolation. Assimilating a number of alien tribal elements, she was the product of a complex ethnogenic process. This took place in the by no means remote past, and was still under way at the height of the feudal period—the classic age, the very period of Confucius—and even much later. In the obscurity of primitive times the clan system produced the "ten thousand city-states" that only briefly antedated the time of Confucius and provided the model for the feudalism of his time. In this it was markedly different from Western feudalism, which was born as the result of the disintegration of a central empire.

A BIRD'S-EYE VIEW OF HISTORY

■ It is easy to imagine the difficulty that must have been encountered by the first Westerners traveling in Asia when they

---

marah; *k'iuen* (archaic Chinese), dog, from the Latin *canis*. These findings were reported in 1936 by Hans Jensen in *Indogermanisch und Chinesisch*, in Arntz, *Germanen und Indogermanen*.

attempted to make the Chinese understand very simple facts of European life; Marco Polo, for example, returning from China, could not make his compatriots believe what he had seen. No fact is isolated: as is too often pointed out today, it is always situated in a context. If one wishes to grasp the life of a doctrine, one must place it in the life of a people—an endless task. What they tell us of themselves is insufficient for the exploration of either. What they conceal, or do not know, is of greater importance. In order to bring this to light, it is necessary to confront objective facts with subjective ones, the first options of historical experience with those of the mind, what is apparent and conscious with what is basic and unconscious. This task is more difficult in the case of Confucius than in that of Plato, for instance; we do not share with the Chinese reader the knowledge of what is conscious and unconscious that is inherent in every language. We must reconstitute an entire universe from its base to its summit. Its two chief dimensions appear to us to be its history and its language. A historical survey is all the more necessary because Chinese thought gambols through historical myths and emerges from them with a kind of astonishing continuity.

Traditional history starts with the Three Venerables, *san huang,* and the Five Sovereigns, *wu ti.* The Three Venerables were Fu-hi, Niu-kua, and Shen-nong; the Five Sovereigns were Huang-ti, Chuan-hiu, Kao-sin, Yao, and Shuen. They represent a golden age, the sacred kings, the founders of civilization. Fu-hi, for example, is regarded not only as the source of a very important book of divination, *Y king,* but also as the inventor of writing and the marriage rite; Shen-nong as the inventor of agriculture; Huang-ti as the inventor of rituals, family names, medicine, etc. Fu-hi, who was the first of them, lived during the fifth millennium B.C.—to be precise, between 4480 and 4365 B.C., according to the traditional dates. This was the period of Obaid in Mesopotamia, and there is nothing implausible in the antiquity of the dates, especially as later historians could not

8

THE COUPLE COMPOSED OF FU-HI (HOLDING THE COMPASS) AND
NIU-KUA (HOLDING THE SQUARE)

have imagined many of the characteristic features of the period.
One would be inclined nevertheless to think that this is a matter
of coordinated cosmogonical myths, interpreted along the lines
of a rational history and arranged in terms of theories evolved
in the fourth century B.C. Thus, in certain unorthodox texts we
see Fu-hi and Niu-kua intertwining their tails, Shen-nong with
the head of an ox, and Huang-ti, the patron of smelters, causing
his daughter Drought to descend from heaven. In any event,
Huang-ti is the patron of the Taoists and Yao and Shuen are
the exemplary sovereigns of Confucianism, and it is on this
basis that they are of interest to us.

This legendary period was followed by that of the Three
Dynasties: the first two divided the second millennium B.C. almost equally between them, and the third virtually took up the

9

first millennium. Nothing certain is known of the Hia Dynasty, the first, which may have set up a group of city-states in Shansi. Its most eminent figure was its founder, Yu the Great, who freed the land from the great waters of the Deluge, and possibly was an expert in irrigation. The Chang, or Yin, Dynasty, which is also known as the Chang-Yin, was the second, and a great deal has been learned about it from archeological excavations. But it is naturally the third that we know best and that concerns us most. The approximate dates (they vary with the chronologies) are: Hia, 1994–1523 B.C.; Chang, 1523–1027; Chu 1027–249.

Excavations carried out at Anyang (or Ngan-yang), in northern Honan, have uncovered temples, palaces, and mausoleums: a whole civilization no longer allows us to doubt the existence of the Changs. Anyang, the Dynasty's first capital, dating from about 1400 B.C., already possessed all the characteristics that marked Chinese civilization. Its writing was already completely developed in its theory (ideophonetic and not ideographic). But it had only two thousand characters, in contrast to the forty thousand of the eighteenth century A.D. The arts of divination and the calendar, both of which play important parts even in modern China, were already in favor. The names of twenty-three of the traditional list of thirty-one kings have been found. In addition, the excavators have discovered bronze and marble sculpture, ivory encrusted with turquoise and mother-of-pearl, cowrie shells from the Maldive Islands in the Indian Ocean, the characteristic mask of the monster, *t'ao-t'ie*, and those famous tripods, caldrons of the Neolithic and even the Paleolithic Ages, that later became sacrificial jars and dynastic urns.

The ancestors of the third, or Chu, Dynasty had long roamed the Chinese Far West in Shensi, north of the Wei, some hundred years before their conquest of China. They paused briefly in the plain of Chu, which may have given them their name, and then settled in Feng, south of the Wei, fifteen miles from present-day Sian (or Si-ngan-fu). They were shepherds and farmers. Al-

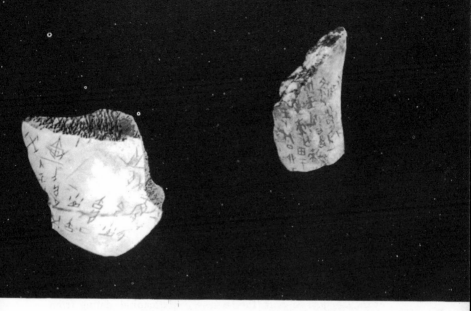

though tradition describes them as Chinese, they probably were not Chinese but members of what the Chinese called the "barbarians." They affected the unification of the Wei basin with the leader known to history as King Wen (the Perfect King), and they conquered the kingdom of the Changs, in the Honan plain, with King Wu (the Warlike King), assisted by his brother, the Duke of Chu. It was because of the duke that what was to have been an ordinary raid for loot was transformed into a durable establishment.

The alien character of the conquerors was still evident several centuries later (eighth century B.C.). There was a certain semblance of discrimination between the conquerors and the conquered:

> *The sons of the east*
> *are called [to service] without encouragement.*
> *The sons of the west*
> *gleam in their splendid attire.*

11

T'ao t'ie MASK

Nevertheless, obeying a well-known law of history, the Chus adopted most of the customs of the Changs.

The Chus established their capital in Hao, near Sian. But, undoubtedly in order to exercise greater control of their recently conquered domain, and as a result of a revolt among their new subjects, they founded twin cities, about ten miles apart, at the entrance to the plain of Honan and the outlet of the narrow corridor through which the Yellow River flowed. One of them, Loyang, or Loyi, was an administrative post before it became the capital; the other was the seat of the Chang nobles. They supported the former heir of the fallen Dynasty of Anyang, in the fief of Wei, in order that he might carry on the

12

TRIPOD-BASED BRONZE URN
(CHU PERIOD)

worship of his ancestors. But he rebelled, thereby giving the land of Sung, lying somewhat farther south, to another Chang peer, the Viscount of Ki. It was the dukes of Sung who were the ancestors of Confucius.

The Chus began definitely to decline into an era of decadence in 771 B.C., when King Yu suffered defeat at the hands of a coalition of barbarians and rebels (the barbarians must have resembled what the Chus themselves had once been). Their power became nominal and purely religious, their title as Sons of Heaven maintained only because of the feudal balance. Their capital was moved eastward to Loyang. This was an illustration of what amounted to a constant in Chinese history: pressure by

13

the barbarians of the west, followed by their conquest of China, which grew greater in consequence. This was the beginning of the era of the eastern Chus and the period of *Spring and Autumn, Ch'uen Ts'yu* (722–481 B.C.), which was followed by that of the *Fighting Kingdoms, Chan kuo* (403–249 B.C.).* Between these two periods, from 479 to 404, there is a visible gap, and Carrington Goodrich has suggested a more rational distribution: Early Chu, Middle Chu, and Late Chu.

The first period was marked by conflict among four large states established on the periphery of the Chinese world, in part through barbarian support. These were Ts'in in Shensi, Tsin in Shansi, Ts'i in Shantung, and Ch'u in the Yangtse (or Blue) River basin. This last seems to have been the least Chinese of all. A north-south coalition was initially mounted against it, led by Tsin. In the second period the coalitions were turned westward against the disconcerting power of Ts'in. The small central states, of course, played the parts of satellites, and their lot was hardly enviable. Lu, for example, where Confucius was born and which had dominated the Chinese northeast until the eighth century B.C., was invaded twenty-two times between 722 and 481. The situation was quite comparable to that of our own era.

In the beginning, this battle for hegemony had had a legal character, if one could call it that: it was in 679 that the supreme title of *pa* was created in favor of Ts'i, which, given the enfeeblement of the royal authority, was charged with leading the Chinese Confederation in its struggle against the barbarians. The title was then held successively by Tsin, Ts'in, and Ch'u before it was abolished in 591 B.C.

At the end of the *Spring and Autumn* period, this struggle among the powerful had extended to the other classes and to individuals. It completely destroyed the old feudal morality. On the other hand, it led to reforms launched by the large states in a spirit of innovation and by the small ones in a spirit of con-

---

* These are in reality the names of two books.

14

servatism. The aristocracy and the people stood opposed to each other. Thus, when Tse-ch'an, an older contemporary of Confucius and a minister of Cheng, embarked on land reforms, although they were under the pressure of military and fiscal needs the aristocracy responded: "Let us take our lands and form a federation! Who will kill Tse-ch'an? We will help that liberator!" But the people retorted: "We have children and adolescents, and Tse-ch'an educates them. We have land; Tse-ch'an has made it fertile." This upheaval in feudal society and its evolution toward the empire initiated the creation of that class of impoverished or landless nobility that, combining with other elements, was to produce the intellectual ferment that went on from Confucius until the end of feudalism.

At the end of the third century B.C., Ts'in, which was a western area of Shensi, accomplished the unity of the Chinese empire by fire and sword and enlarged it to almost its present boundaries as a result of the superiority of cavalry over chariots. From then on, Chinese history followed the profile of a "Russian mountain." The powerful dynasties of Han, T'ang, etc., were interrupted by the Middle Ages, characterized at first by fragmentation and then by the barbarian invasions. Recent Chinese history between 1911 and 1949 seems to have repeated the same pattern, regardless of the ideological position that one may adopt toward the government of mainland China.

THE LIFE OF CONFUCIUS

■ Confucius was born in Tsu, a little town in the principality of Lu (located in the southwestern part of the modern province of Shantung, in northeastern China). This event occurred in winter, on the twentieth day ("the day of the eleventh rat") of the tenth month of the twenty-first year of Duke Siang of Lu, or, as it was also known, the twentieth year of King Ling of the sovereign house of Chu. By our solar calendar, according to the calculations made by Eul-su Yun, this would be August 27, 551 (or 552) B.C., around the time of Buddha in India, Py-

17

thagoras in Greece, Nebuchadnezzar and the Babylonian captivity in Mesopotamia. Socrates and Empedocles came into the world a few years after Confucius had left it.

Lu was a small principality nestled between two powerful states, Ts'i on the north and Wu on the south, both of more or less barbarian origin. Lu's neighbors on the west were Wei and Sung, two other small central states of Honan. Both resembled Lu in their position in the feudal world, the origins of their princes, the antiquity of their civilization, and the seniority of their place in the Chinese Confederation. Lu, however, was more oriented toward the seacoast and seemed less civilized. It bordered on the province of Honan, the cradle of China, and it looked toward the sea beyond the somber rocky cliffs from which rose the sacred mountain of T'ai chan with its eternally green cedars. Confucius had contemplated this mountain in his childhood and he was to recall its image in the hour of his death. But Lu's greatest honor was the fact that it had been founded by the Duke of Chu, whose ghost was pleased to haunt the countryside. He had been the wise counselor of the first kings, some six centuries earlier. Confucius would have liked to perform the same function for the princes of his own day.

Confucius is the Latinized form created by the Jesuits of K'ong fu-tse, Master K'ong. His family name was K'ong, his personal name was K'iu, and his appellation—more precisely, his public personal name—was Chong-ni, or Ni the Younger.

His father is supposed to have been Shu-leang Ho, the son of Po-hia and the grandson of K'ong Fang-shu, the governor of Fang and the first of his line to have emigrated to Lu. He himself is supposed to have been governor of Tsu. (Confucius was sometimes designated under the name of "the son of the man of Tsu.") In 556 B.C., accompanied by two other military officers and at the head of three hundred men, he executed a sacrificial night mission: a successful attack against the encirclement organized by a Ts'i army. He also distinguished himself on another occasion—the siege of Pi-yang in 536 B.C. During

18

the fighting, he made his way into the besieged stronghold through a vertically sliding door that had deliberately been left open and that could be closed by being lowered. He and his men had barely entered when the door closed again. Fortunately, he was strong enough to be able to lift the door with both his hands and thus save his comrades in arms and himself. In both cases he was serving as an officer of junior rank.

Supposedly Confucius was of royal lineage, a descendant of the Chang kings. When the Chu Dynasty replaced the Chang, the victors gave the land of Wei to the last prince of the fallen dynasty in order to provide him with a place where he could continue the ancestral sacrifices. But he rebelled and an appeal was then made to the Viscount of Ki, the son of the last king but one, though by a subordinate wife; he had lived in retirement—it might be said, in the opposition—under the reign of his brother, the last king of Chang. His is supposed to have

been the credit for handing over to the new dynasty the Great Rule of government of the Changs in nine articles, the *Hong-fan*. In recompense for this he received the fief of Sung in southern Wei.

The first appearance of the name K'ong occurred in the eighth century B.C. with K'ong Fu-kia. By this time it was separated from the reigning line of the Dukes of Sung by five generations, and custom decreed that its bearer adopt a new name in order to distinguish him from the ruling family. It was Fu-kia's bad luck to have a wife whose beauty seduced Prime Minister Hoa Tu, and Tu had him assassinated in 710 B.C. But the widow committed suicide on the way to the palace, strangling herself with her girdle. This gave rise to a protracted enmity between the two families. Finally Fu-kia's great-grandson had to move to Lu as an expatriate. It was K'ong Fang-shu who was given the command of the fortress of Fang, probably because of his noble birth. (But the fact seems less than definite, since Fang belonged to the powerful Tseng clan, unless Fang-shu was in the service of that clan.) Fang was about six miles northeast of the capital of Lu, situated on a plateau almost a half-mile east of the modern K'iu-fu. Tsu was in the eastern outskirts of the capital; this means that the father of Confucius did not live inside the city's walls, as did the other nobles of his time.

Shu-leang Ho's first wife was a daughter of the Sheu family. She bore him nine daughters. A subsidiary wife bore him a crippled son, Möng-pi, whose public name was Pö-ni. But daughters and a son whose body is not physically intact are not suited to the perpetuation of the worship of the ancestors, a very important matter in Chinese society. So, at an advanced age—more than seventy—he married a girl of the Yen family who was young enough to still be wearing a pin in her hair—she was fifteen years old. An "unbalanced" marriage, Sseu-ma Ts'ien observed chastely. That was the term applied to any marriage entered into by a man under the age of sixteen or over the age of seventy-four or by a woman under the age of four-

GENEALOGY OF CONFUCIUS

Viscount
Ki of Wei
(*Prince of Song*)

Thong-seu
(*Prince of Wei, Ki's younger brother*)

Ki
(*Duke of Song*)

Chen
(*Duke Ting*)

Hong
(*Duke Min*)

Hi
(*Duke Siang*; d. 908)

Fang-seu
(*Duke Li*)

Fu-fu Ho (d. 893;
killed by his brother, Fang-seu)

Song-fu Chu

She-tse Cheng (?)

Ch'eng Kao-fu (eighth century B.C.;
humble and scholarly, studied ancient poetry)

K'ong Fu-kia (d. 710;
master of the horse, killed by Hoa Tu)

Mu-kin-fu
(*reduced to the rank of ordinary nobility*)

Kao-y or K'i-fu

K'ong Fang-shu

Po-hia

Shu-leang Ho (d. 553)

K'ong K'iu, *or* Confucius (551–479 B.C.)

21

teen or over the age of forty-nine. It was from this Yen family that Confucius' favorite disciple, Yen Huei, who is occasionally likened to St. John, was descended.

Father Yen called his three daughters together and spoke to them in this wise: "This is how it is with the commander of Tsu. His father and grandfather are mere noblemen. But his ancestors are descended from our holy kings. He is ten feet in stature and his courage is remarkable. I wish to make an alliance with him. Although he is old and his character is austere, there is no reason to hesitate. Which among you, my three children, wishes to be his wife?"

The two eldest daughters did not reply. But Cheng-tsai, the youngest, stepped forward and said: "Our father has commanded us. I will obey. Why ask questions?"

So Cheng-tsai was presented at the ancestral temple of her husband's family, three months to the day after she had entered the family for the first time. After the ceremony, she was filled with dread lest she be unable to conceive a male child, given the advanced age of her husband, and she went secretly to pray in a temple on Mount Ni-k'yu. This was the origin of Confucius' name "K'yu," a hill, or, more precisely, a hollow mound. In Sseu-ma Ts'ien's opinion, the name was derived from the shape of Confucius' skull, which was somewhat flat on top and higher around the edge, like a shallow dish. Others said that he had a high, slightly concave forehead, and that this was the source of his name.

As the young woman was climbing the slope of Ni-k'yu, the leaves of the trees and plants stood up; they bowed gracefully and deferentially when she went down again. (This is one of the few legendary elements in the story of Confucius.) In a dream that night Cheng-tsai saw the Black Lord (Lord of the Waters), who told her: "You will give birth to a son, a wise man, whom you will deposit beneath a hollow mulberry tree."

During her pregnancy, she fell one day into a state of drowsiness or "waking dream." She had a vision of five old

22

men who seemed to have the essences of the five planets. With them they were leading an animal that looked like a calf, but it had a single horn and it was covered with scales, like a dragon. The animal knelt before her and regurgitated a piece of jade on which was written: "A child born of the essence of the water will succeed the decadent Chu Dynasty as a king without a crown."

Cheng-tsai tied a ribbon of embroidered silk round the animal's horn. Then the vision vanished. When she told her husband of this strange occurrence, he said, "That must be the unicorn, the *k'i-lin.*"

When the time for her confinement was near, she asked her husband about the existence of a place called the "hollow mulberry tree." Shu-leang Ho told her that there was indeed a grotto by that name on the hill to the south. "I am going to shut myself up in it," she informed him.

He was surprised, but after she had explained he ordered

THE *k'i-lin* ANNOUNCING THE BIRTH OF CONFUCIUS

AS HE WAS BEING BORN, THE
AIR ECHOED WITH HEAVENLY MUSIC

the requisite arrangements made. In the instant in which she
gave birth to her son, two dragons were standing guard to the
right and left of the hill; two female spirits appeared in the
air and sprayed the grotto with perfumes; a spring of hot water
appeared and at once disappeared, so that the new baby's body
might be washed. The air echoed with heavenly music and a
voice was distinctly heard to say: "Moved by your prayers,
Heaven has given you a holy child."

Sseu-ma Ts'ien, it should be observed, did not accept this
legend, which was summarized briefly in the *Luen yu*. In this
version the grotto of the hollow mulberry tree was replaced,
undoubtedly by design, by the family house. The tree, indeed,
aroused suspicions of some illicit romance. The term still has
the same meaning in literature today; it is reminiscent of the
orgiastic festivals of primitive peasant times which were held in
groves of mulberry trees.

Some vestiges of the story may still be traced today among the mountain peoples of North Vietnam and southern China, and, in a strange survival, in the village of Lim in the North Vietnamese delta. There, at a certain time in the year, boys and girls meet beside the rivers or in the fields to sing and offer their love in a tournament of alternated songs that is reminiscent of the ancient sexual jousts. These are rites for the fertilization of the soil and perhaps, as in the case of the dance of the ear of wheat in Assam, they date from the matriarchal period, which the patriarchal customs of the Chinese aristocracy made every effort to eliminate, not without difficulty.

K'ong: PERIOD OF CONFUCIUS   SEVEN CENTURIES LATER   MODERN CHARACTER

These customs are also evoked by the name of Confucius. The character *K'ong* means "hollow"; it is made up of two graphic components that used to mean "swallow's egg." This recalls the springtime, when boys and girls went in groups to look for swallows' eggs. But it means also that the family of Confucius was descended from the kings of Chang, whose first ancestor was "born of a swallow's egg."

Marcel Granet has very skillfully analyzed the sociological content of this myth and of Confucian hagiography in general. They were derived from late theories (approximately fourth century B.C.) on the correspondence between elements, the five elements symbolized by the five old men. The Changs reigned through the virtues of water, hence the Black Lord, Hö Ti, water corresponding to black, but also the skull of Confucius in the shape of a hollow mound.

I have no intention here of examining this complex analysis. Let us conclude merely by saying that the biography of Confucius had to undergo a certain treatment, fortunately in an

25

incomplete fashion, in order to enter into the mold of later orthodoxy.

CHILDHOOD AND YOUTH

■ Few details are known about Confucius' childhood, which was poor and obscure. His father died when Confucius was three years old and his very young mother, widowed at the age of eighteen, had to rear him on the meager yield of the strip of land usually awarded to the widow of an official without means; he himself had to work in various manual trades. He went hunting and fishing, but he did not use nets or traps, and he never shot an arrow at a bird that was sleeping on a tree (*L.Y.*, VII, 26). Later he said to an exalted personage who was amazed at his numerous talents, "When I was young I was of humble condition; that is why I had to learn to do many things. But these are matters of little import; does the wise man need to know how to do many things?" (*L.Y.*, IX, 6).

He derived a certain pleasure from handling sacrificial objects in his childhood play. There is nothing surprising in this. The little provincial courts, removed from the power politics of the great states of the time, were much concerned with ceremonies and rituals. The child must have seen more of these in Lu than elsewhere; moreover, the capital was a little place, and what happened at court was immediately known in the town. At the age of seven he was perhaps the pupil of a teacher from Ts'i. He tells us merely that he applied himself to study at the age of fifteen, and he describes his intellectual itinerary thus: "At fifteen I applied myself to study; at thirty I was solidly established; at forty I no longer doubted; at fifty I knew the decree of heaven; at sixty I understood what I heard; at seventy, following the inclinations of my heart, I did not transgress the rule" (*L.Y.*, II, 4).

Where and under whom did he study? We do not know. Schools in those days had various names: *hio, hiao, siu, ts'ang,* etc. Some were in villages, others were in the capital. There is nothing to preclude the supposition that he studied in the academies of the nobility, for his teaching was inspired by them. These were a kind of seminary in which the young nobleman was trained for military and court life between the ages of ten and twenty. The school, established outside the city or the village in the northwestern suburbs, was isolated by a circular or semicircular moat. Its curriculum was a clue to its spirit: history, literature, arithmetic, handwriting, music, dance, and deportment (ritual), as well as military exercises: shooting with the bow and driving the chariot. To all these things was added instruction in the three cardinal virtues: feudalistic loyalty to the prince, the master, and the father. Curiously, dance, music, archery, driving the chariot, handwriting, and arithmetic were classified among the six trades, or techniques.

At the end of his studies, the young noble obtained his bonnet of manhood. He had let his hair grow and on the appropriate day (determined by the achillea) in the second month of the year the ceremony was held in the eastern building in the presence of family and friends.

"On this excellent, this solemn day," the young noble was told, "the bonnet is placed on your head for the first time. May your childish feelings be banished; act in conformity with your quality as a man grown; may your old age be happy; may your happiness accumulate in splendor."

The young man thereupon received his adult or public name, *tse,* which is occasionally translated as "appellation" for lack of a better word, and which henceforth took the place of his given name, *ming.* Thus, Confucius' personal name was K'yu and his "appellation" was Chong-ni.

But before the new name was bestowed, there was a ceremonial proclamation: "The rites and the ceremonies have been accomplished. In this auspicious month, on this solemn day, I

27

proclaim your appellation. Now this appellation is wholly auspicious; it is a name that befits a patrician who wears a top-knot; it is fitting for you who have arrived at man's estate; receive it and keep it forever." *

THE START OF HIS CAREER

■ At the age of nineteen, Confucius married a girl of the Kien-kuan family, which came from the principality of Sung, where his own family had originated. A year later she bore him a son, Li, the carp—in honor of the occasion Duke Chao had presented Confucius with a carp, and in appreciation of the prince's favor he gave his son this name (to which was added later the appellation of Pö-yu, Carp the Elder, for often the appellation was a paraphrase of the personal name). The fact that the duke had sent Confucius a carp showed that in spite of his poverty he still enjoyed honorable rank in the capital of Lu. Indeed, this was no minor favor, and there had been times when men had struck bronzes to commemorate similar circumstances.

Confucius also became the father of a daughter, though it is not known when. He married her to Kong-ye Ch'ang, a man who was believed to understand the speech of birds. At the time of the wedding the bridegroom was wrongfully imprisoned, but this did not deter Confucius from permitting the marriage.

At about the same time, he was made superintendent of the public granaries. A year later, he was appointed to the supervision of the posts to which the sacrificial bulls and sheep were tethered. At that time, according to *Meng-tse* (V, ii, 5), he said, "I endeavor to keep my accounts accurate, that is all. I

---

* Cf. H. Maspéro, *La Chine Antique* (Paris: new edition, 1955), pages 110–1.

THE DUKE HAD PRESENTED A CARP TO CONFUCIUS

attempt to make certain that the bulls and sheep are fat and healthy, that they grow, that is all. It is a mistake to speak of lofty matters from a humble station." This doctrine was to be repeated in the *Chong Yong:* act in complete accord with the situation.

In his twenty-second year, in 530 B.C., Confucius opened a school in Lu. Each student paid according to his means. "Whenever anyone came to my school bringing the customary presents, even if they were only ten slices of dried meat, I never refused my teachings" (*L.Y.*, VII, 7).

He insisted on a predisposition of will and intelligence. "I cannot compel understanding in him who does not endeavor

30

with all his heart to understand. I cannot teach proper speech to him who does not make an effort to speak. If I have shown him one corner of a question and he has not seen the three others, I refuse to teach him" (*L.Y.*, VII, 8). "If someone does not say: 'How is it to be done? How is it to be done?' what can I do for him?" (*L.Y.*, XV, 2).

This was really a school and not a "philosophical school"; its program was largely that of the official institutions. Nevertheless, the summer curriculum with its open-air activities was thrust aside in favor of the winter curriculum. The pupils studied and practiced the rites, music, and poetry; they studied history, the careers of the kings in the *Shu king*, and Confucius added the history of his own country, known as *Ch'uen Ts'yu*. He taught antiquity and nothing else. "I transmit, I do not

CONFUCIUS AT HIS POST AS
SUPERVISOR OF THE PUBLIC GRANARIES

invent" (*L.Y.*, VII, 1). This was not a declaration of principle, but it may have been an advertising slogan, for the young noblemen did not come in search of anything else, and they were inclined to be distrustful of innovators.

One can picture the young teacher, already esteemed for his scholarship at the age of twenty-two, sitting on the steps of the terrace of the main room in front of the inner courtyard, his face turned toward the south, like a prince receiving his vassals. He was like the feudal lord before his dependents, or the Hindu *guru* who in his own person possesses the secret and the ultimate guaranty of his knowledge. The pupils remained at his door: *men-jen*, the men of the doorway, the disciples. The tendency of Chinese teachers has not altered perceptibly, and anyone who knows them can easily imagine the scene.

Two years later, in 528 B.C., Confucius' mother died. She was barely forty years old, and the end of this woman, who is hardly mentioned in history, is not unaffecting. Confucius wanted to bury her with his father, in the same grave in Fang, the place where the family's ancestors had first settled in Lu. But his father had been dead for more than twenty years, and Confucius did not know where his grave was. Through an old woman, Wan-fu, he learned that the tomb was at the crossroads of the Five Fathers, near Tsu. It was a temporary grave: according to Chinese custom, the body would be moved after a few years to a place determined by geomantic means to be appropriate. So Confucius moved the bodies of his father and mother to Fang and buried them there, side by side. Above the grave he erected a mound four feet high. But this was counter to the practice of the ancients, and when his disciples who had remained behind returned later to tell him that a storm had destroyed his monument, he must have viewed this as a punishment by the gods. "Ah," he observed, "they did not do this in antiquity!" And he burst into tears.

"In ancient times," he added, "one did not create a mound above the grave. But I am a man who belongs to the north and

33

A YOUNG TEACHER ALREADY ENJOYING
A REPUTATION AT THE AGE OF TWENTY-TWO . . .

the south, to the east and the west. I need something to preserve my memory." This was an expression of his sentiment, or a presentiment of his wandering destiny.

He wore mourning for his mother for the prescribed twenty-seven months—three times the period of gestation. Five days after his mourning had ended, he began to play his lute, and it was only five more days later that he was able to sing to the accompaniment of his favorite instrument.

In the meantime, while he was still wearing the girdle of mourning, the head of the powerful Ki clan gave a banquet for men of rank. Confucius should not have attended if he was to conform to the rites. But he appeared at the feast. Yang Hu, the Ki family's officer, and a man of redoubtable ambition, insulted him: "The head of the Ki family is giving a banquet to men of rank. He would not demean himself to give you a banquet." Confucius retreated.

During the two or three years that followed the mourning period—which was a time of inactivity—he must have continued learning and teaching. Toward the end of this time, he went to Master Siang to improve his knowledge of music. He was extremely responsive to music and, like all Chinese, he ascribed a singular virtue to it. It had the capacity to reveal the soul—at least, to a sister soul—and to cure it, to assure order and peace for society and the universe.

After ten days of study, Master Siang said to him: "You can go farther."

"I, K'yu," Confucius replied, speaking of himself by his personal name in order to stress his humility, "have practiced the melodies, but I have not yet grasped the numerical proportions."

"You can go farther," Siang repeated.

"I do not yet understand," K'yu confessed, "what man it is that is behind that music."

"The majestic melody that you play contains some profound thought, the joyous melody that you play carries some high hope or some distant thought."

34

"Now I understand who that man was. His shadowy apparition is black; in stature he is exceedingly tall. His look is that of the sheep who gazes into the distance; his heart is that of him who reigns over the realm of the four points of the horizon. If he is not King Wen, who is he?"

King Wen was the founder of the Chu Dynasty. So it was the music that this king had invented six centuries earlier. And here again political concern is present.

In 524 B.C. the Viscount of T'an, a minor leader of a minor state lying 110 miles to the southwest of the capital of Lu, went to Lu. The duke gave a banquet in his honor. An excellent orator, the viscount asserted that the rituals of the early sovereigns, going back to the legendary Huang-ti, had been faithfully preserved in T'an. Confucius was extremely interested and could not rest until he had learned from the viscount all that was to be learned about his country. In spite of uncertainty as to its authenticity, the story reveals a number of things: that Confucius was invited to the court, that the whole society was deeply interested in rituals and completely oriented toward the past. This was not exactly the case in the great peripheral states of more or less barbarian origin: they hewed to a realistic, cruder morality of power; the others, in contrast, clung to an archaic ideal of civilization. A parallel with our own time exists.

Two years later—Confucius was then in his thirtieth year, the age, he said, at which his mind was solidly established—Duke King of Ts'i went to Lu with his wise minister Yen Ying (or Yen P'ing-chong), whose fealty in friendship won praise from Confucius. Duke King sent for Confucius and asked him: "In the past, Duke Mu of Ts'in [who had died just a century earlier] held a small territory in a remote region [Shensi]. How did it come to pass that he was able to win hegemony?"

"Although the Duke of Ts'in had a small kingdom," Confucius replied, "his determination was great; although he dwelled in a remote area, his conduct was just and upright. He himself elevated the officer of the five rams to the rank of grand officer; he himself freed him from the bonds that were strangling him and conversed with him for three days. Then he entrusted the government to him. He could even have achieved royalty; it was a small matter that he obtained hegemony."

This was a proposal that the duke employ wise men, select them himself, and treat them with deference. Duke King was pleased with the reply. Engaged in conflict with the noble clans in his country, he seemed to be seeking support from the "sages," the intellectuals of the time—an indefinite and, in the last analysis, anything but powerful class. He appeared to be looking for them in Lu, which he regarded as a protectorate. Besides, his prime minister, Yen Ying, had come out of such circles, a man of modest origin born in the barbarous regions of the seacoast. Although in actuality he was working for the noble clans, his presence at the head of the government was nevertheless a sign of the times.

In 518 B.C., Möng Hi was near death. He was one of the chief ministers of Lu and the head of one of the country's three powerful clans. Mindful of the frustrations that his ignorance of the rites had cost him seventeen years before, he sent for his son, Möng Y.

"Knowledge of the rites," the father asserted, "gives a man his foundation. Without it he cannot hold his ground. I have heard it said that there is a man whose knowledge of them is perfect: he is K'ong K'yu. He is descended from the holy men. And, although his line is extinct in Sung, his ancestors included Fu-fu Ho, who renounced the ducal throne in favor of his brother, and Ch'eng Kao-fu, who was renowned for his knowledge and his humility. Tseng Hi has remarked that if wise men of great virtue do not attain the high place in the world that is rightfully theirs, it is certain that among their descendants there will be a man endowed with insight. These words hold true for K'ong K'yu. After my death you will have to go to him and study the rites."

THE JOURNEY TO LOYANG

■ So it was that Möng Y and the son of another powerful family, Nan-kong King-shu (or Nan-kong Kua), presented themselves as disciples at Confucius' gate. Through their intercession, Confucius was enabled to study rites and music in Chu, where, it was believed, they had been preserved in their pristine purity. The Duke of Lu gave him a chariot, two horses, and a servant, and he departed with Nan-kong King-shu.

In spite of the political decline of the kings of Chu, which reduced their domain to nothing, their capital was a religious center to which imposing memories were attached, like medieval Rome or the Vatican. Later a poet was to sing of its "broad and lofty roads," and Shao Yung, in the eleventh century A.D., was to say, "I am happy to be a man and not a woman, a Chinese and not a barbarian, and to live in Loyang, the most beautiful city in the world." This was essentially what was said by a contemporary of Confucius, Jung Chi-k'i.

Even in those times the journey must not have been very arduous. Undoubtedly the travelers took the road along the dike, which followed the bank of the Yellow River, for then, as now, vehicles required this route. As soon as they were out of sight of the severe lines of T'ai shan and the low hills of Shantung, they were at once in the rich Honan plain. At the elbow turn of Kaifong, they turned eastward, still following the great river. They were able to contemplate the opaque, opal-colored waters of this river, which fed the countryside as it followed a gentle slope that made its course extremely capricious. (Until 1194 it emptied into the sea north of the Shantung mountain range; then it assumed a southerly course, resuming its northerly flow in 1853; it had wandered over a distance equivalent to that between the English Channel and the Rhône delta, and, of course, swept away everything that lay in its path. It inspired great dread in the dwellers on its banks, who worshiped it in the guise of a black serpent kept in a temple and probably fed occasional human victims. At certain flood times a girl would be married to the Count of the River, Ho Pa.)

As soon as Confucius and his companion were within sight of the foothills of T'ai Hang, they were in Loyang. This city, it will be recalled, was founded approximately six centuries earlier by the Duke of Chu. But it did not become the capital until the decline of the royal house had begun. Until then the royal capital was in Hao, near the modern Sian in the Chinese "far west," Shensi, on the far side of the corridor through which the Yellow River flowed. The region was well situated strategically, and it was from there that both the First Emperor and Mao Tse-tung were to come; it was where all the dynasties had maintained their capital as long as they were able to hold out against the assaults by the barbarians.

Even today one can still see the tombs of the first Chu heroes on a little plateau that looks out over the valley of the Wei. In the misty distance they are like truncated earthen pyramids, twenty-five to thirty feet high, with a periphery three times that figure at the base, according to the calculations of Herlee G. Creel. The surrounding villages have cared for them for more than three thousand years. The tombs of Kings Wen and Wu, the Duke of Chu, and their successors, Kings Ch'eng and K'ang, are embraced within an area of approximately two and one-third square miles. There they sleep, Creel said, in "majestic silence." To anyone who knows the history of China, the sight cannot be other than impressive. To the north one can see the mountain from which the first Chus came; to the south there is the distant silhouette of the Ts'in ling chain.

It is not difficult to imagine the state of mind in which Confucius and Nan-kong King-shu arrived in Loyang. They had the opportunity to admire the royal palace, the outer enclosure of which measured more than two miles in length. It formed a square, each side of which included three gateways surmounted by sentry towers. The buildings must have been of the size of those of the Chang Dynasty, a thousand years earlier, as it has become known to us through the excavations at Anyang: twenty-five to thirty feet broad and eighty to a hundred feet long. Perhaps the roofs did not slope so low as those of modern times, and they were not turned up at the ends. (This phenomenon is of southern origin, and at this time the area south of the Yangtse River was not yet Chinese.) Perhaps they were already decorated with fabulous animals such as the unicorn. The walls, the pillars, and the roof trees must have been polychromatic, the roof trees jutting out. The floors were of packed earth.

The palace is described in the *She king:*

> *Near the graceful curves of those shores,*
> *With the southern hills so peaceful in the distance,*
> *[The palace] solid as bamboo roots,*

40

PAVILION WITH COLUMNS (HAN PERIOD)

[Its roof] like the rich summit of a pine . . .
Long are the roof trees of jutting pines,
High are the many pillars.

Through one of the gates that opened to the south, one entered the courtyard, which contained among other things the
nine Dynastic urns, at the end of the hall used for solemn audiences on the eastern side. Following one of the nine longitudinal
avenues (there were also nine lateral ones), one went through
another door, which led into another court with another audience chamber, and it was only after the third door that one
arrived at the royal apartments and the garden.

Confucius examined the mounds where, when it was time for

41

the ceremony of *kiao,* the Son of Heaven made his sacrifices to heaven after he had fasted and purified himself. He inspected the mounds consecrated to the worship of the soil and the seed, *shö tsi,* which were the symbols of the royal domain and later of the state. They were surrounded by chestnut trees planted in the time of the Chus, trees that were supposed to suggest the idea of the severity of punishment. He visited the Hall of Light, *Ming t'ang,* in which the vassals were received. During an audience, the king kept his face turned to the south, from which comes the *yang.* His arms rested on stools adorned with jade; at his left stood a minister who assisted him in the reception, a kind of minister of protocol, and at his right was the Great Scribe. The visiting lord prostrated himself at a distance; then he rose, and remained standing in the middle of the court. When the king had spoken, the scribe wrote down his words. The visitor prostrated himself again and then withdrew, walking backward. Confucius could see on the walls the portraits of the sovereigns of the early ages, Yao and Shuen, the august founders of the human race, under whose patronage he had placed himself. But what emotion, what silent reverence filled him when he

42

stood before the portrait of the Duke of Chu, the founder of Lu, by whose image he was haunted. The duke, at that time the regent, was shown holding King Ch'eng, still a child, on his knees and receiving the lords of the four quarters of the Chinese universe.

"Here," Confucius said, "we see how the Chus became great. As in a mirror, we read the reason for the present in the past."

If earlier, in the ancestral temple in Lu, he had asked "questions about everything," one can imagine the questions that his piety toward the past made him ask of himself in this environment.

He visited Ch'ang Hong (who, according to the *Huai-nan-tse,* died in 492 B.C.) for enlightenment on music. As a rule, the music masters were blind, and on more than one occasion Confucius displayed great respect and active compassion toward them. But apparently Ch'ang Hong was not blind, if we are to believe the opinion of Confucius: "I have observed more than one sign of the wise man in Chong-ni. His eyes are like a river, and his forehead is a dragon's. He is nine feet, six inches tall, and he looks like T'ang the Victorious. When he speaks, it is in praise of the ancient kings. He follows the way of humility and courtesy. He has heard many things, and he remembers them. The range of his knowledge seems inexhaustible. Do we not see in him the emergence of a wise man?"

Lao-tse, or the Old Master, was at that time the archivist, or keeper of the royal treasure, in Loyang. Confucius was eager to question him about the rites. When Confucius spoke to him of the sages of the past, Lao-tse said, "The bones of all those of whom you speak have crumbled into dust; only their words remain. When the wise man finds work to occupy him, he travels in a chariot; otherwise he walks, carrying his pulpit himself. I have heard it said that a good merchant carefully conceals his goods and acts as if he had nothing, and that a perfect sage makes himself appear a fool. Put aside your arrogant manner and your insatiable desires, your affected demeanor and your excessive ambitions. None of that is of any use to you."

In his *She ki*, Sseu-ma Ts'ien recorded this exchange in Chapter 63, which is devoted to Lao-tse. In Chapter 47 we find a somewhat different version: "I have heard it said that the rich and powerful man gives people riches when he sends them away, and that the good man gives them words. It would be impossible for me to be either rich or powerful, but secretly I claim to be a good man, and I will send you away with these words: 'He who is intelligent and a sharp observer is near his death, for he criticizes men accurately; he whose mind is knowledgeable and broad puts his person in peril, for he unmasks the flaws of others. He who is a son cannot own himself; he who is a subject cannot own himself.' "

After the meeting Confucius was at first unable to speak; then he confided to Nan-kong King-shu: "I know that the bird flies, that the fish swims, that animals walk; but animals can be taken with the net, fish with the line, birds with an arrow attached to a cord. As for the dragon, I know nothing, except perhaps that he ascends to heaven carried by the clouds and the wind. Today I saw Lao-tse. He is like the dragon."

The conversation between Confucius and Lao-tse is mentioned on at least five occasions in the *Chuang-tse*, with some variations: for example, that Confucius had gone to Loyang in order to place his manuscripts in the royal library, and his traveling companion was Tse-Lu; or that he had journeyed south at the age of fifty-one; or that Lao-tse was in the cataleptic state well known to the shamans and the Taoists, the state known as a "spiritual journey."

In any event, the story was very well known in the Han period, the two centuries before the Christian era; that is, in the time of Sseu-ma Ts'ien. In fact it is to be found carved in stone.[*]

---

[*] See Chavannes, *Mission archéologique*, figures 137, 169, 1223, and 1235, and *Corpus des pierres sculptées Han*, of the Sinological Center of Peking, Volume I, plates 87, 89, 129; Volume II, plates 150 and 165.

CONFUCIUS MEETS LAO-TSE
(HAN PERIOD)

In one of the bas-reliefs, Confucius and Lao-tse are shown, and facing Confucius, from the same direction as Lao-tse, there is a child holding a broom or (according to Michel Soymié) a wheel at the end of a pole: the symbol of a vehicle.* This remarkable child is Hiang T'o. It has been thought that the child was none other than Lao-tse himself, wisdom assuming the dual antithetical guise of the old man and the child. He is the *puer senex* so well known to Latin literature.

Confucius met him during a journey, the time of which is not

---

* Cf. *Journal Asiatique*, 1954, parts 3–4.

known, that is believed by some to have taken him eastward to
the foot of Mount King; others hold that he was traveling westward to Shensi. Hiang T'o, alone in the midst of other children
at play, was building a miniature fortress beside the road.

"Why do you not get out of the way of my chariot?" Confucius asked him.

"I have always heard it said," the little boy replied, "that it is
the chariots that go around cities, and not cities that move out
of the path of chariots."

Confucius stepped down into the road. "How is it that you
are so wise at so early an age?"

"Three days after birth," Hiang T'o replied, "a child can
distinguish between his father and his mother; three days after
birth a hare can run across the fields; three days after birth a
fish can swim in rivers and lakes. It is natural. Has wisdom anything to do with it?"

Confucius asked the boy his name and appellation and where
he lived, and the child told him. (In an ancient version, the boy
said that he had no name and lived in the house of the wind.)
Confucius suggested: "I should like to walk with you. What do
you say?"

"At home," Hiang T'o said, "I have an august father, whom
I have to serve, a loving mother, whom I have to feed, a wise
elder brother, whose counsels I have to follow, a weak younger
brother, whom I have to teach, and an illuminated teacher, under whose guidance I study. How could I find the time to take
a walk with you?"

"We are going to level the world. Do you want to?"

"It would not be right to level the world. On the one hand
there are high mountains, on the other there are rivers and
lakes; on the one side there are princes, on the other there are
slaves. If we level the mountains, the birds will no longer have
a shelter; if we fill the rivers and lakes, the fish will no longer
have a refuge. If the princes are driven out, the people will argue
forever trying to find where good and evil lie. If there are no

46

more slaves, who will respectable people command? The world is so tremendous. How can it be leveled?"

Confucius then asked the little boy a number of riddles. Hiang T'o propounded others in his turn. Finally he asked Confucius, "How many stars are there in the sky?"

"Let us talk about what is within our reach," Confucius answered.

"How many hairs are there in your eyebrows?" the boy countered.

Confucius smiled but said nothing. Then he turned to his disciples and declared: "The young are to be feared. How can one be certain that the generations to come will not be the equals of those of today?" *

I have reduced the story of the meeting between Hiang T'o and Confucius to its essence, following the very well-known modern version intended for Chinese children but read by adults as well. There are longer and more complicated versions in Chinese, Mongol, Japanese, Thai, and Vietnamese. The end of the conversation clearly evidences a criticism of the Confucian idea of the *happy medium*: Confucius knew neither what was remote nor what was close. There is also an allusion to his wandering life, his vain desire to reform and pacify the world: *p'ing* means both *to level* and *to pacify*. But it is possible that the criticism has a touch of irony with respect to the Confucian idea of the family.

There was, moreover, a reciprocal impregnation between the two great Chinese schools, and the story of Hiang T'o was current in Confucian circles from the time of the Hans. Both schools appear to have drawn on the same fund of folklore.

---

* In another version he is supposed to have said, "Precocious children will not amount to much later." The first remark is a quotation from the *Luen yu* (IX, 22) used in a specific contest that alters its meaning, for the remark by Confucious as quoted in that work is repeated without any clue to the circumstances.

Not only is it the meaning of every humanism to be open to all that is human, but Chinese syncretism tends consistently to eliminate doctrinal frontiers, and through the ages the two schools seem to represent complementary rather than opposing attitudes.

POLITICS IN LU:
THE USURPATIONS OF THE POWERFUL

■ Confucius returned to Lu during the same year in which he had departed. Now he was like a *hadj*, a Moslem who has been to Mecca. His prestige was growing, and the number of his disciples mounted, it seems, to three thousand, a figure that is certainly exaggerated, rounded out in terms of mystic ideas about numbers.

For some time the situation of Lu, like that of the other small central states in the Chinese Confederation, had been tragic. The Chinese world of that time was divided into two opposing coalitions: a Northern League, headed by the state of Tsin, and a Southern League, headed by the state of Ch'u. Lying on the border between the two but belonging to the Northern League, Lu was continually in danger of offending one or the other; at the same time, it had to protect itself against a third large state which was declining: Ts'i, its immediate northern neighbor. (Not to mention another large state, Ts'in, far to the west, which a few centuries later was to emerge as the third thief in the fable.)

Just as the "three families" seemed to be the wards of the state of Ts'in, the Duke of Lu seemed to be protected by T'si. This clearly showed Lu's satellite condition. In addition Duke Chao was the target of many harassments by the large states. In 539 B.C. he went to pay homage to Tsin. When he reached the bank of the Yellow River, Duke P'ing of Tsin refused to receive him and rudely sent him packing. The whole country of Lu covered its face in shame. In 527 B.C. he was detained in Tsin against his will. Ts'in, in the "far west" of Shensi, also subjected him to innumerable affronts. In 534 B.C. his southern neighbor, King Ling of Chu, ordered a festival to commemorate the completion of the terrace of Chang-hoa; he gave Duke Chao a precious object as a gift, then thought better of his generosity and took it back by trickery.

Lu's internal situation was also confused and troubled. Power was in the hands of three noble clans, the "three Huans"—that is, the three descendants of Duke Huan, whom the *Luen yu* calls the "three families." These were the Ki-suens, the Shu-suens, and the Möng-suens, or simply the Kis, the Shus, and the Möngs. The Kis were the most powerful. They owned the larger part of the territory and had their base at Pi, about forty-five miles east of the capital; it was a formidable stronghold. The Shu clan had established its base about thirty-five miles west of it, and the Möng clan was fifteen miles to the north, on the border between Ts'i and Lu. The three clans enjoyed all the revenues of the state. In 537 B.C. they also shared the monopoly of military power, whence the division of the army into three corps instead of the original two. Similarly, all high positions fell to them by inheritance. Moreover, by sending presents to the ruling clans of Tsin, they obtained the protection of the leader of the northern coalition against the duke.

To the great outrage of Confucius, the chief of the Ki clan arrogated to himself the prerogatives of the Son of Heaven, offering sacrifices to T'ai shan, the sacred mountain, and using the royal hymn, hitherto reserved for the kings of Chu, in the ceremonies in his ancestral temple. And, whereas the impoverished duke had to dismiss his ancestral temple's dance troupe in 517 B.C. and the musicians who played for his four daily meals had to emigrate to other countries, the Kis had a pantomime troupe of eight ranks of eight dancers each. (The vassal princes were entitled to only six dancers each, and the *tai fu*—

grand officer, the rank of the Kis—to only four.) We may find these problems of protocol laughable, but they were of great importance, especially to Confucius, in a social environment in which public functions had a religious significance, in which the king was a priest-king—in short, in which there was no distinction between *kchattrya* and *brahman*, between the warrior and the priest.

The crisis came in the ninth month of 516 B.C., the year after Confucius had returned to Lu from his journey to Loyang. During a cock-fight an angry quarrel erupted between P'ing of Ki and Chao-po of the Hu clan. P'ing had sprinkled mustard on his rooster's wings and Chao-po had armed his rooster's spurs with metal. The duke seized on this opportunity to rally the other clans against the Kis and, with the help of the young men of this warrior class and the wandering knights and scribes who were beginning to appear at this time, he made a surprise attack on Ki. Under siege, Ki mounted to a tower of his fortress and attempted to negotiate. He offered to pay indemnities, to leave the city and live in the outskirts, or to exile himself to his estate with whatever property he could carry in five chariots. The duke was adamant. In desperation Ki turned to the two other clans, pointing out to them that if he were destroyed the duke would lose no time in attacking them. The Shus saw the danger and executed a quick shift of allegiance: Möng's troops surged out of their base and the duke had barely time to escape to Ts'i.

EXILE IN TS'I

■ As a good monarchist, Confucius could not do less than follow his prince into exile. On his way to Ts'i he encountered a woman weeping and crying out heart-rendingly beside a

50

grave. Tse-Lu went to ask her what was grieving her.

"My husband's father was eaten by a tiger," the woman explained, "and then the tiger ate my husband, and now he has eaten my son."

"Then why do you not move to another place?" Confucius asked.

"Because here there is a government that does not oppress the people."

Confucius was deeply impressed by her reply. "See, my disciples," he said, "a bad government is more to be feared than the tiger."

Later, in allusion to this story, it was to be said that when the empire is in disorder even an ordinary woman cannot live in peace. In other words, nowhere is it possible to escape the effects of politics, whether in some invisible corner of the empire of China or in our fragile ivory towers. Here already was a theory of commitment.

As he entered the outskirts closer to Ts'i, Confucius observed a boy carrying a jar. The boy's eyes were bright and he walked with a confident step. Going part of the way with him, Confucius saw that he had an upright heart as well. In his enthusiasm, he cried to his driver, "Speed the horses! Speed the horses! I can already hear the *shao* music."

This was the music that was believed to have come down from the wise sovereign Shuen, and its practice was faithfully continued in Ts'i. For three months Confucius studied it with pious zeal, so intensely that he was no longer aware of the taste of his food. "I would not have believed that the composer of these songs had attained to such perfection," he said.

Fidelity to one's prince was a virtue that was highly esteemed in the feudal world, for feudalism was based on it. Moreover, in his own realm Duke King of Ts'i was facing problems similar to those that had confronted his counterpart in Lu: the struggle against oligarchic clans. Again there were three of these: the Ts'ueis, the Ch'engs, and the T'iens, the third of whom had only recently acquired power and wealth. In 548 B.C., thirty years before Confucius arrived in the country, Ts'uei had gone as far as to kill Duke Chuang, who had maintained an illicit relation with his wife. By inheritance, the clans of Ch'eng and Ts'uei shared the posts of Minister to the Right of the Throne and Minister to the Left of the Throne. But a conflict broke out between them; the Ts'uei clan was completely eliminated and the Ch'engs were left with the monopoly of power. Then, corrupted by it, they gave way to the T'iens, whose recent ancestors were not even natives of the country. The T'iens were clever enough to keep themselves in the background. Yen Ying, the popular Prime Minister, was in fact their man. One of the "wise counsellors," he was from the seacoast, a man who, much like Confucius, had come from nothing (as his world viewed such matters). The duke's policy was not unlike that of Henri IV against the great feudal barons, or that of Louis XIV, who formed an alliance with the merchant class.

This state of affairs undoubtedly explains why Confucius was granted the favor of a number of audiences with the Duke of Ts'i. Consulted by the duke on the art of government, he replied: "Let the prince behave as a prince, the subject as a subject, the father as a father, the son as a son" (*L.Y.*, XII, 11).

This was a castigation of the usurpations that were current. The duke approved, and remarked rather innocently that if it were otherwise, even universal abundance would be of no value. In another situation, Confucius was to clarify his thought, justifying a legitimist concept of the social order—that is, a conservative utopia—with the observation that if the primary source of power was transferred from the legitimate hands of the king (of Chu) to those of his vassals, and then to those of the nobles, as far as essential matters were concerned—the rites, music, and war—power would not survive long (for the usurpers): ten generations in one case, a few years in another (*L.Y.*, XVI, 2). This remark must have been made after

the Ki clan, which had expelled the Duke of Lu, had itself been
overthrown by one of its officers, Yang Hu, a few years later,
in 505 B.C. When Tse-Lu asked him what he would do if the
Prince of Wei bestowed power on him, and Confucius replied,
"Rectify the names" (*L.Y.*, XIII, 3), it must not be interpreted
as "Rectify the concepts," in terms of a philosophical notion;
it must be viewed simply as the expression of that same conservative utopia of an idealized feudal character.

In another instance, Confucius urged economy on the duke,
"the use of riches with moderation." This was undoubtedly the
reaction of a man who had come from a poor country against
the luxury that reigned in Lin-tso, the capital of Ts'i, a state
that had held hegemony over the Chinese world during the
first part of the previous century, that had accumulated wealth,

54

that possessed a thousand four-horse chariots, and had always encouraged trade in salt and fish. In the Confucian school there was to be a certain distrust of trade, which was to be ranked lowest among all occupations, below agriculture and artisanry.

Duke King wanted to present Confucius with a hereditary estate, that of Ni-k'yu. Earlier, when he had just arrived in Ts'i, he had been offered the city of Lin-k'yu. But Confucius felt at that time that since he had not yet performed any service for the duke, it did not behoove him to accept; in fact, he was seeking some employment in which he could utilize his talents, not an income. This time it was the Prime Minister, Yen Ying, Minister of Ts'i, who opposed the idea. Confucius' monarchism did not please everyone, especially the grand officers. It must be conceded, however, that Yen Ying's portrait of Confucius, though something of a caricature, was remarkably apt:

> The *ju* [the scribe, the man of letters] is a sophist who cannot be taken as a model or a criterion. It would be out of the question to allow the people to be governed by such men, arrogant and guided only by their own opinions. Placing great importance in the ceremonials of mourning, they abandon themselves to affliction and dissipate fortunes in lavish funerals: it would be out of the question to allow them to regulate morals. They are garrulous, and they wander from place to place in search of loans: it would be out of the question to allow them to run the state. After the great sages appeared, when the house of Chu began to decline, the rites and music fell into decay and were full of gaps. Therefore Confucius increases outer forms and fine appearances; he complicates the rites for going up and down, the rules for walking quickly and with the arms outstretched. Many lives would be too few to complete the studies that he prescribed; years of effort would not enable one to examine all these rites in depth. If, Prince, you de-

sire to employ him to reform the customs of Ts'i, that will be no way of placing the welfare of the people in the first rank of your concerns.

When he had heard this, and just before he received Confucius, Duke King said to his ministers: "I cannot treat him as one would Ki. I will treat him in a manner midway between Ki and Möng." Even this meant attributing considerable rank to Confucius—the position of a *tai-fu*. Then, perhaps sensing the resistance of his lords, the duke added, "I am old. I would not be able to put his doctrine into practice."

Confucius saw that it was time to go. He was disillusioned when he left. "A reform," he said, "would raise Ts'i to the level of Lu; but a reform would place Lu on the way" (*L.Y.*, VI, 22).

In what year did he return to Lu? Was it 515 or 514 B.C., two years after his arrival in Ts'i? Or was it 509 B.C., the year in which Duke Chao of Lu died in exile in a little border city in Ts'i? In any event, there was virtually no mention of Confucius for many years, and one can picture him engaged in study and bringing order into the works of antiquity, *She king* and *Shu king*, which were the texts from which he taught.

REBELS AGAINST USURPERS

■ The death of Duke Chao put an end to the interregnum of the "three families," and the throne of Lu passed to Duke Ting. It was during this interregnum, when they were at the apex of their power, that the three families planted the seeds of their downfall. First of all, one usurpation leads to another, and it was quite possible that the idea of legitimacy attaching to the person of a prince in exile had in it something that could touch hearts. As early as 530 B.C., as the result of some minor irritation, Nan K'uai, an officer of the Ki clan who was in command of the base of Pi, had revolted against P'ing of Ki and attempted to restore this important stronghold to the possession of the ducal house. This would have destroyed the power of the Kis at its source.

In 505 B.C., the head of the clan, P'ing (who, out of deference, was also called P'ing-tse), died, and Huan succeeded him. Over an ostensibly trivial question—whether to bury the jewels of the ducal house, which he had used improperly during the interregnum, with P'ing; Yang Hu favored doing so—a quarrel broke out within the clan between two factions. Yang Hu, a sort of keeper of the palace for the Kis, seized all the leaders of the clan, including Huan, led them to a platform at the southern gate of the capital, and forced them to swear to accept the expulsion of Kong-fu Wen-po, one of the most popular members of the clan.

This success emboldened Yang Hu, and in 501 B.C., on the pretext of offering sacrifices to the ancestor of the ducal house, he summoned Huan-tse to the ceremony with the intention of sacrificing him—killing him—in the courtyard of the ancestral temple. The day before, he had mobilized all the chariot forces in the country. This was what alerted the leader of the Möng clan. A cousin of Yang Hu was assigned to escort Huan-tse to the ceremony, but on the way Huan succeeded in winning over the driver, who agreed to head for the Möng estate at top speed. A confused battle broke out; it was decided by the arrival of Möng troops from their base, Ch'eng. Yang Hu had barely time to flee, carrying off to Ts'i the "crown jewels" and the ducal bow, the symbol of power that had been given by the King of Chu to the founder of the principality.

The impression arises that Yang Hu had attempted to employ the legitimist myth on his own behalf by sacrificing Huan to the ancestors of the ducal house. Undoubtedly for the same reason, he had tried to gain the sponsorship of Confucius, whose position as a legitimist had certainly been reinforced after his voluntary exile in Ts'i and by his attitude of prudence and reserve during all these years.

The affair went back to some period before Yang Hu's flight. Since Confucius had not gone to visit him, Yang Hu tried to force him to do so. To this end he sent Confucius a young pig as a gift. Confucius chose for his visit of thanks a time when Yang Hu was not at home. Unfortunately, he ran into Yang Hu on the way, and Yang Hu said, "I have something to discuss with you. Does he who conceals his treasure and leaves his country in disarray deserve to be called beneficent, *jen?*" When Confucius replied negatively, Yang Hu continued, "Does he who takes an interest in public affairs and lets opportunities to guide them pass by deserve to be called prudent? The days and the months go by, the years do not wait for us."

"Very well," Confucius said, "I will accept a post." *

Even though on the basis of pure legitimist principle Yang Hu owed fealty to the duke alone, the course taken by affairs, at least since the middle of the *Ch'uen Ts'yu* period, tended to assimilate the relation between client and patron to that existing between subject and prince and between vassal and sovereign. Rebelling against the Kis, Yang Hu naturally had to appeal to the ducal authority. He was looking for an alibi that it seemed Confucius could provide for him. Both men had one thing in common: they were opposed to the usurping power of the *tai-fu.* Furthermore, in periods of instability government was eager to seek recruits among new men already surrounded by a certain reputation, especially when the recruit in question was one of the representatives of that class of impoverished minor nobility, knights, warriors, and educated scribes, the *shes,* who seemed at that time to be making a forceful entrance

---

* The chapter of the *Luen yu* (XVII, 1) in which this story is told uses the name of Yang Huo. But it is quite clear that it is the same man who is meant.

on the stage of history. As for Confucius, while he had no desire for a frontal clash with Yang Hu, he was obviously avoiding compromising his own career with a soldier of fortune.

It is impossible to conclude from this anecdote, as some have done,* that Confucius had in fact taken service with Yang Hu. If he had not done so, however, he could not have kept his promise to Yang Hu. It is understandable that the story was embarrassing for the orthodox commentator of the *Luen yu,* who intimated that Confucius merely was interested in finding employment—when the right time came. But we are not compelled to share the scruples of the commentator, and we are well aware that a revolutionary situation is of necessity very fluid. Besides, Confucius was not the rigid personality

---

* Cf. H. Maspéro, *La Chine Antique,* 1955, page 377.

that has been supposed. On one occasion, when a promise had been extorted from him by violence, he declared afterward that "the gods did not hear it."

Furthermore, immediately after Yang Hu's flight, Confucius went through the same experience with Kong-shan Fu-jao (also known as Kong-shan Pu-niu), one of Yang Hu's allies, who in spite of his associate's defeat had continued to occupy the important stronghold of Pi, the Kis' family base. He too appealed to Confucius, and once more Confucius hesitated visibly. He was on the point of accepting Kong-shan's invitation (*L.Y.*, XVII, 5). But loyal Tse-Lu was outraged: "You must go nowhere. What reason have we to go to Kong-shan?"

"Did he who has sent for me do so without a purpose?" Confucius asked. "If I find employment, I shall be able to establish a kingdom of eastern Chu."

We shall never know the real reason on which Confucius acted. Duty is never too clear in confused situations. Undoubtedly, he still cherished the dream of restoring the legitimate authority of the Chus and the princes of Lu, and perhaps, in the desperate state in which Lu was, he looked on Kong-shan in his impregnable citadel of Pi as the man who could accomplish his project. It has also been suggested that he felt somewhat compromised with Yang Hu. In the end, Confucius did not go.

He was then fifty years old, the age that in China automatically invested one with a kind of seniority, the rank of *ai*, an elder (at forty Confucius had been classed in the category of *ch'ang*, a strong, fully educated man, and, as such, qualified for responsibility). Perhaps, too, this was the age at which the desire to act and accomplish was becoming more urgent and more impatient.

Several years afterward, moreover, about 493 B.C., during his peripatetic life, Confucius was again subject to the same temptation. Here we anticipate the chronology because the matter serves to clarify his intention and perhaps his desire as well.

60

Pi Hi, the commander of the stronghold of Chong-meu, had also revolted against the *tai-fus* of the state of Tsin, the clans of Fan and Chong-hang—a phenomenon that was becoming increasingly frequent at this period. He sent for Confucius, who was preparing to accept the invitation when once more Tse-Lu resisted. "Master," he said, "I have heard you say in the past that the wise man of quality does not associate himself with one who is engaged in a guilty enterprise. Pi Hi is a rebel and you intend to go and see him. What does this mean?"

"I did indeed say that. But is it not said also that what is hard cannot be used for rubbing and that what is white cannot be blackened by paint? Am I like a bitter gourd that is hung but not eaten?" (*L.Y.*, XVII, 7).

THE ASCENT TO POWER

■ Let us go back to 500 B.C., after the flight of Yang Hu. Peace came back to Lu, but it was very precarious. The oligarchic clans had found themselves on the edge of disaster, and certainly they had had to negotiate with Kong-shan Fu-jao. The duke had been able to regain some authority. Perhaps at this time he was in a better position to employ Confucius, who seems to have succeeded in holding himself aloof from events. It is beyond all doubt that for some time—as we have seen from the instances cited—Confucius had been much sought after, partly because of his legitimist beliefs, partly because of his reputation for knowledge and wisdom.

In 501 B.C. Duke Ting appointed him governor of Chong-tu. The description of his government given in the *Kia yu* makes one think of that of a golden age under the earliest sovereigns. He assured food supplies for old and young, settled the duties to be borne by everyone, established a system of measures, ordered the segregation of the sexes in the streets, and regulated funeral ceremonies. In order to follow the example of the ancients and achieve his antiquity-minded utopia, it was forbidden to erect mounds or plant trees on graves. It was said that things dropped in the streets no longer were picked up by those who passed.

After a year the duke asked Confucius whether the method of government that had been successful in Chong-tu could be applied with the same results to the country as a whole. When Confucius said that it could, the duke made him superintendent of public works and, not long afterward, Minister of Justice.

In the spring of 499 B.C., Confucius had the opportunity to apply his talents to the diplomatic domain. The occasion was a peace conference in Kia-Ku between Ts'i and Lu. He took part in it as a kind of protocol officer. Opposite him was Yen Ying, the Prime Minister of Ts'i, who in the past, it will be remembered, had already come into conflict with him. Yen Ying, although a dwarf, was a famous statesman, whose feeling toward Confucius was what a man of action, governing the affairs of a great state, could nourish toward a man whom he considered to be overburdened with the ceremonial and apprehensive in appearance. Ts'i had recently seized certain territories belonging to Lu, and at Kia-Ku he wanted to make a show of strength that would impress the duke; if necessary, Yen Ying was prepared to take him prisoner.

Since the occasion was a peace conference, the duke was prepared to go to it without any martial array, in ordinary chariots. But Confucius objected. "Your subject has heard it said," he told Duke Ting, "that when there is peace to be talked, one should make preparations for war, and when there is war to be talked, one should make preparations for peace . . . Take with you your marshals of the right and the left."

After their exchange of greetings, the two princes took their places on a platform to which access was gained by climbing three steps. Just as they were about to exchange libations, an officer of Ts'i stepped forward and played the music of the *Four Points of the Compass.* Immediately helmets capped with feathers and skins, pikes, halberds, swords, and shields surged up everywhere, accompanied by the roll of drums and the blood-chilling cries of a band of strangely dressed savages brought by Ts'i from its coastal regions.

Confucius speedily went up the first two steps, but not the third, and stretched out his arms. "Our princes are holding a friendly meeting," he said. "What is the music of the barbarians doing here? It is not thus that Ts'i could command the princes of the Flowered Kingdom. Such conduct in the face of the gods can only draw down misfortunes."

Everyone turned toward the Duke of Ts'i at this unexpected intervention by the master of ceremonies of Lu. Duke King was ashamed, and waved his flag to order a halt to the savage dance. But at that moment, and probably in accordance with a previously concerted plan, another officer of Ts'i ordered the music of the *Inner Palace* played. Immediately the place was filled with jesters, dwarfs, clowns, and grotesquely arrayed singers.

Confucius raised his arms again, this time saying, "When vile fellows disturb a conference of their lords, they deserve to be chastised. Let them be seized and punished according to the rules!" Punishment by proxy was nothing uncommon in those days: this was in fact a threat to the Duke of Ts'i himself. He saw that his ruse had been exposed and that Lu had certainly made preparations for war, and he was afraid. The show of force was turning against him.

Finally, Lu agreed to supply three hundred war chariots for expeditions ordered by Ts'i. In return, Ts'i agreed to return the territories that it had seized from Lu. On the advice of an official who felt that a noble ought not, like the common man, to excuse himself merely in words, Duke King of Ts'i wanted to make a genuine gesture by returning to Lu the illegally annexed lands.

A number of critics have challenged the facts of this story, but they are in complete accord with the spirit of the China of that day, still susceptible to ritual influences fundamentally linked with magic behavior patterns. Nor does the more or less conventionalized description of Confucius' government of Chong-tu adduce any evidence against that government. Chinese diction is no more descriptive than it is analytic. It proceeds in an allusive fashion, through references to historical precedents, and it frequently resorts to stereotyped formulae—to the cento, as Marcel Granet points out. The accuracy of the details can be determined in a conclusive fashion only through a critical examination of the texts based on the study of the language and the style.

It has also been argued (cf. Maspéro) that since by inheritance the duties of the superintendent of public works belonged to the Möng clan and those of the Minister of Justice belonged to the Tsangs, it is most unlikely that Confucius should have held either post. It is this fact that caused James Legge to assert that Confucius was merely an assistant in both departments. But as we have seen, after the revolts of Yang Hu and Kong-shan Fu-jao five years earlier, the position of the oligarchic clans was no longer very firm. It was quite possible that on the duke's return the legitimism of Confucius placed him in an advantageous position. It seems reasonable to me, then, to follow the traditional account, which has in its favor the fact that it was accepted by Sseu-ma Ts'ien. This is the conclusion that was reached as well by Professor Shigeki Kaizuka of Japan in a recent book. In every case the future was to show a certain logic among events, as well as Confucius' adherence to his line of conduct.

It was the success of the conference of Kia-Ku that made it possible for Confucius to play a determining part in the court of Lu. In order to unseat the power of the noble clans, he made Lu withdraw from the northern coalition, and he adopted a position that we today would call neutralist. It is

65

known that Tsin, the leader of the coalition, was protecting the clans.

Following the same project, he persuaded the "three families" to demolish their strongpoints of Pi, Heu, and Ch'eng, from which their power came and from which, too, their troops could at any time invest the capital. In the beginning, clearly, these had been positions established for the defense of the borders, but, as always in Chinese history, in the end the periphery had borne down on the center. After the rebellion by the commander of Pi, who comported himself there like an independent lord, like the "war lords" of modern China, the leaders of the three clans were more inclined to accept the proposal of Confucius.

The work of demolition was entrusted to Tse-Lu, who at that time entered the service of the Kis with Jen Yeu. The business began quite well. The Shu-suens themselves destroyed their base at Heu. But when the outer walls of Pi began to come down, the population of the region, under the pressure of that same Kong-shan Fu-jao whom we have already encountered—and this was the proof that he was operating there like an independent lord—and Shu-suen Che, rose and marched on the capital. Duke Ting and the chiefs of the three clans had to flee to a tower. Finally the rebels were defeated at Ku-mie, and Kong-shan Fu-jao had to travel the well-beaten path of flight into Ts'i.

Then the Möng clan refused to destroy its base at Ch'eng, arguing that it was necessary for the defense of the northern border against a possible invasion from Ts'i. The duke was constrained to lead an expedition against them, but it was a failure.

At about this time, we are told, Ts'i, made uneasy by Lu's gains under the direction of Confucius, attempted to divert the minds of the country's leaders from their duty. To this end it sent as a gift a company of eighty female dancers and musicians of surpassing beauty, as well as twenty splendid

66

four-horse chariots. When these marvels arrived at the gates of the capital, they excited so much interest that Huan-tse of Ki disguised himself in order to go secretly to see them. For three days the duke let the state's business slide. Tse-Lu thereupon urged Confucius to resign his office. But Confucius waited a little longer, until the *kiao* sacrifice, the sacrifice to heaven. When the duke showed himself to be negligent in the performance of such important rituals, Confucius decided to depart.

It is probable that this moralistic tale conceals political facts of a graver nature. The internal equilibrium of a feudal state is constantly changing. It had changed after the demolition of Heu and again after the flight and elimination of Kong-shan Fu-jao, the more or less independent commander of Pi. Now the clan of Ki was once again the master of its traditional base. It no longer had the same reason to back the policy of Confucius, who by now had become an intruder.

THE WANDERING YEARS

■ Confucius went away regretfully, followed by his disciples. This was in 497 or 496 B.C., and he was about fifty-six years old. In a kind of ritualism that is to be observed in other situations, he departed slowly from the soil of his fatherland. He was about to embark on thirteen years of peregrinations. His melancholy found words:

From afar I look at the land of Lu,
Mount·Kuei hides it from my view.
I carry no ax in my hand;
What can I do against Mount Kuei?

It is not certain that these lines really were written by Confucius, but the mountain in question was certainly an allusion to Huan of Ki.

Confucius traveled first in the direction of the neighboring state of Wei. At Y, the border city, the official assigned to the city's defense asked to be introduced to him, and noticed the sadness of his disciples. "Why do you grieve at your master's loss of his post?" he asked them. "The world has long since lost its way. Heaven is using your master as a bell with a wooden clapper to warn the people" (*L.Y.*, III, 24). One is reminded of Hamlet's lament, "The time is out of joint."

When Confucius arrived in Wei, he lodged at first with an older brother of Tse-Lu's wife, Yen Chu-yeu. It must be assumed that his reputation was solidly established, for on the whole he was very well received by the princes. Duke Ling of Wei was generous. He asked Confucius what he had been paid in Lu and gave him the same amount: sixty thousand measures of grain. But the *tai-fus* were less cordial; undoubtedly they were perturbed by his legitimism. After about a year, feeling that he was being watched, and fearing some conspiracy among the aristocracy, Confucius left Wei for Ch'en, a state to the south of what is today Honan.

He broke his journey at K'uang, near the modern Kaifong, at the point where the Yellow River turns east. At the walls of the city, his driver made the mistake of remarking, "I have gone through this breach before": the local people thought that Confucius' group was made up of troops who had besieged the city in the past. In addition, Confucius was mistaken for Yang Hu, who had committed atrocities; the people of K'uang wanted to make him and his companions pay reparations. Tse-Lu was

69

ready to fight, but Confucius, beginning to play his lute, prevailed on him to be calm. Seeing the anxiety of his disciples, he now for the first time voiced his own view of his mission: "Was not King Wen's doctrine entrusted to me after he died? Heaven would not have made me his heir if it had wanted that doctrine to vanish from the face of the earth. And if heaven does not want that, what can the people of K'uang do to me?" (*L.Y.*, IX, 5).

Yen Yuen, or Yen Huei, the favorite disciple, had remained behind, and it was just in this hour of peril that he belatedly arrived. Seeing him again after so much danger, Confucius cried, "I thought you were dead!"

Yen Yuen's reply was moving in its devotion: "O Master, as long as you are alive, how can I dare to die?"

Apparently, Confucius gave up the journey to Ch'en and went back to Wei. He stayed with a *tai-fu*, Kiu Po-yu, a man who is described to us (*L.Y.*, XIV, 26) as one of great modesty in spite of the importance of his position. By now the year was 495 B.C.

In the court of Wei there was a favorite of the duke, Princess Nan-tse, who had been born in Sung. She was notorious for her depravity, and there was a prevalent humor that she would not stop even at incest. She expressed a desire to see Confucius: "The sages of the four points of the compass who have not been ashamed to desire brotherly relations with our prince have never omitted visiting me, a mere princess."

After much hesitation, Confucius had to defer to her wish. He prostrated himself before a curtain behind which the princess sat. She replied to his greeting several times, and he could hear the bells of her girdle tinkling. She answered him according to the rites, Confucius conceded. But Tse-Lu was angry nevertheless, and irritated that his master had consented to visit a woman of bad reputation. On this occasion Confucius could only appeal to heaven: "If I have done wrong, may heaven refuse me! may heaven refuse me!"

70

Somewhat later, Duke Ling requested his company for a ride. The duke and the beautiful Nan-tse were sitting in the first carriage and Confucius was in the one that followed. The populace shouted, "See how virtue runs after beauty." Confucius was ashamed, and he sighed, "I have yet to meet a man who loved virtue as much as outer splendor" (*L.Y.*, IX, 17).

Once more he left Wei for Ch'en. He traveled through Ts'ao in order to reach Sung. The commander of that state's cavalry, Huan T'uei, wanted to kill him for some unknown reason. While Confucius and his disciples were talking beneath a tree, Huan had the tree felled. For the second time, Confucius voiced his mystic belief in his mission (*L.Y.*, VII, 22). Then, it would appear, the Master and his disciples were driven westward in disarray, toward the state of Ch'eng. A man from that country came to Tse-Lu and said, "At the eastern gate there is a man who stays there like a dog on a burial day."

This remark was repeated to Confucius, who replied: "Outer appearance matters little. But it is quite true that I do look like a dog on a burial day."

The entire group arrived in Ch'en just at the end of 495 B.C. Confucius spent three years there, living with a supervisor of the fortifications. In 494 he had an opportunity to demonstrate his knowledge of antiquity in areas that were not related to his usual teachings, and to provide us with some idea of what science was in those days.

In a battle between the states of Wu and Yue, both lying in the region of the mouth of the Yangtse River, a hill was trampled down, and in the rubble enormous bones were found lying in a chariot. Some kind of animal? A prehistoric beast? A giant man or ancestor of man? * The explanation by Confucius,

---

* A recent article (*Discovery*, October, 1956) by the English archeologist Cornwall discussing a report by the Chinese scholar W. C. Pei to the Chinese Academy of Sciences stated that forty teeth have been found belonging to an anthropoid nine and a half feet tall. Such a creature would be a contemporary of Peking Man, who lived five hundred thousand years ago.

naturally, was historical-mythical. He said that in the time of the legendary King Yu there had been a meeting of the *shen*, the divine (a word that apparently was used to designate both the gods of the mountains and rivers and the priests who served them), on a hill called Kuei Ki. One of them, a giant named Fang Fong—it was not known whether he was a god or a priest—arrived late. He was killed by Yu and his body was left unburied. This was supposed to be the origin of the bones. (Here one notes an interesting distinction between two classes of priests: the divine, charged with the cult of mountains and rivers, and the others, who were merely dukes and marquesses charged with the worship of the gods of the soil and the harvest. All were subject to the king. This corroborates the sacral character of public office in primitive China.)

On this same occasion we find Confucius speaking of *ti*, giants, and *tsiao-yo*, very small men who existed in his time. In the latter instance he probably meant Negritos of southern China, who were mentioned in the texts until the third century B.C., or pygmies who, according to the *Kuo-ti she* of the seventh century, lived south of Ta Ts'in—in other words, south of the Roman Empire. They lived in caves and were afraid of being devoured by cranes.

At this time Ch'en was the victim of frequent attacks by its neighbors, particularly Wu. Confucius resumed his journey toward Wei. At P'u the governor had rebelled against Wei. Confucius was detained; he was released only on his oath not to continue his journey. He did not keep his promise. When he was reminded of the fact by the good Tse-Lu, who was always outspoken, he said, "That was an oath extorted by force. The gods did not hear it."

Duke Ling of Wei went out to meet Confucius and greeted him with deference. But he did not heed the sage's counsels. "If there were someone who would employ me," Confucius said, "in one year I would make progress; in three years I would succeed."

It was at this point in his life, it will be remembered, that

he compared himself with "a bitter gourd that is hung but not eaten," hesitating in the urgent conviction of his mission at the call of a man who had revolted against the noble clans of Tsin.

One day, as he was playing on the sounding stone, a man passed by his door, carrying on his shoulders a basket in which to gather grass. He was a wise man who lived in seclusion. "The man who is playing the sounding stone has a heart," the wise man said. Then he added, "But he is fruitlessly stubborn. Since no one knows him, why does he not resign himself? 'If the ford is deep, I will cross it bare-legged; if it is not deep, I will raise my garments as high as the knee' [a quotation from the *She king*]."

This is an illustration, at once curious and typical, of the way in which the Chinese employ the verses of the *She king*, a fashion similar to that of westerners with the Bible.

The remark was repeated to Confucius, who said: "How cruel he [that man indifferent to the life of the world] is. There is nothing difficult in living as he does" (*L.Y.*, XIV, 42).

This incident is quite characteristic of Confucius.

74

Wearied by his lack of employment in Wei, he decided to go to Tsin, the leader of the Northern League. But when he arrived at the bank of the Yellow River he learned that Teu Ming-tu and Shuen-hoa had died. Approaching the water, he said: "How beautiful this broad river is! If I do not cross it, it is the will of destiny."

"Allow me to ask you why you say that," Tse-Kong said.

"Teu Ming-tu and Shuen-hoa were wise grand officers of the realm of Tsin. As long as Chao Kien-tse had not achieved his ends, he needed those two men; then he killed them. I have heard it said, 'When the full wombs are opened so that the young may be killed prematurely, the unicorn comes no longer to the walls; when pools are drained, the dragon no longer preserves the harmony between *yin* and *yang;* when nests are overturned in order to break the eggs, the phoenix does not glide down.' This means, 'The wise man avoids what is harmful to those who are like himself.' "

Acting on this, Confucius went back to Wei. One day the duke questioned him on military problems. "In matters of the meats and the jars of sacrifice," Confucius replied, "I have long been engaged in study, but as for the art of arraying armies, I have never examined it" (*L.Y.*, XV, 1). Absently, the duke watched the flight of a goose.

The next day Confucius left Wei for Ch'en, where he spent the whole of 491 B.C. At this time he received news from Lu. Duke Ting had died the year before; a few months later, in the autumn, Ki Hoan, the leader of the Ki clan, had also died. On his deathbed, as if in remorse, he told his son Ki Kang, "When you become counselor of Lu, do not fail to summon Chong-ni [Confucius] to your side."

But Kong Che-yu pointed out to Ki Kang, "In the past your father granted an employment to Confucius but did not keep him for the full term; in the end he was the laughing stock of the nobles. If you take him into your service and do not keep him until the full term, you too will be in the same ridiculous situation."

"Whom should I summon?"

"You must call Jen K'iu."

Confucius was convinced that Jen K'iu, also known as Tse-Yeu, was going to be employed in an important position. At this moment he felt a desire to return to his native land, from which he had now been absent for several years. "If only I could return! if only I could return!" he said. "My disciples are ardent but negligent. They cultivate virtues with elegance and perfection, but they do not know how to balance them."

More precisely, on another occasion he observed that each of his disciples excelled in different virtues, even surpassing himself, but that all of them lacked the capacity to relate and harmonize them. This was the theory of the *happy medium* or *golden mean* that was to be elaborated by his grandson. "To overstep bounds is no less a fault than not to reach them" (*L.Y.*, XI, 15).

Accompanied by his disciples, Confucius left Ch'en in 490 B.C. for Ts'ai, a small principality dependent on the large state of Ch'u, the leader of the Southern League. Ch'en was subsequently attacked once more by Wu: it was one of those unhappy countries pressured and compressed by both the Northern and the Southern Leagues. The King of Ch'u went to its aid. Informed that Confucius was between Ch'en and Ts'ai, he ordered gifts sent to him with an invitation to appear before the court. This alarmed the *tai-fus* in Ch'en and Ts'ai—further proof that the legitimist position of Confucius was well known—and they ordered a blockade thrown up round him.

For seven days Confucius was without food. Weakened by hunger, his disciples could not even stand up. The master's calm angered Tse-Lu, who cried, "Is the wise man to be stripped of everything?"

"The wise man may indeed be distressed. But in such a situation the ordinary man can no longer contain himself," Confucius replied. Tse-Lu understood and blushed (*L.Y.*, XV, 1).

Aware of the vexation among his disciples, Confucius under-

76

took a kind of examination of conscience among the school. To Tse-Lu he said: "The *She king* asserts: 'We are not tigers and rhinoceroses that we should remain in desert places.' Why am I in such a position?"

"In my opinion," Tse-Lu replied, "it is because our goodness is not sufficient to cause men to believe us; it is because our wisdom is not sufficient that men do not follow our precepts."

"What do you think, Yeu? If a good man were necessarily believed, then there would have been no Pö Yi or Shu Ts'i" [they had vainly remonstrated with the tyrant Cheyu-sin, the last of the Chang kings, and then gone to die in the forest out of loyalty to the Chang Dynasty]; "if the wise man were followed, there would have been no kings' sons like Pi-Kan" [a prince of the blood who had been executed because of his protests to the last of the Chang kings]:

Then Confucius turned to Tse-Kong, who said, "Your wisdom is exceedingly great. That is why there is no one in the empire who will accept you. Master, you ought to lower [the level of your teachings] a little."

"A good farmer sows," Confucius answered, "but he is not sure that he will reap. A skillful artisan is not sure that he

will please. The superior man puts wisdom into practice; he upholds the basic rules; he observes the principles; he has no assurance at all that he will win their acceptance. But if you say that in order to gain acceptance one must not practice wisdom, then your aspirations are not very high."

Then it was time for Yen Huei, the favorite disciple, to speak. "Your wisdom is most lofty; that is why there is no one in the empire who will accept it . . . If we do not practice wisdom we ought to be ashamed, but when, having practiced it, we are not employed, it is the lords who ought to be ashamed."

This response pleased Confucius. "O son of Yen," he smiled, "if you had great riches, I would be your overseer."

Perhaps this examination of conscience in the midst of peril had the value of comforting the disciples. Tse-Kong was dispatched to the King of Ch'u. Soon a rescue force appeared and delivered the besieged group.

Confucius then went to the capital of Ch'u, where the king tried to give him an estate comprising seven hundred families. But the great lords opposed the plan, and it failed.

Confucius remained in Ts'ai through 489 B.C. and beyond. Then he settled at She, a city that was also dependent on Ch'u, the head of which had wrongfully arrogated to himself the title of duke. This official consulted Confucius on the art of government, and Confucius told him, "A good government brings happiness to those who are near and attracts those who are far away" (L.Y., XIII, 16).

Actually, in this area as in everything else, he had little faith in maxims of a general nature (L.Y., XIII, 15; IV, 21). He merely counseled vigilance. If one had achieved virtue in oneself one would know the art of government. If one were perfect, as King Shuen had been, then it was enough to face the south in the proper fashion, in order to ingest the emanations of the yang, and this would keep the empire in order (L.Y., XV, 4).

On another occasion the governor of She said to Confucius, "There are upright men in my country. If a father steals a sheep, his son does not hesitate to testify against him."

"The upright men in my country behave differently," Confucius retorted. "The father conceals the faults of the son as the son conceals those of the father" (*L.Y.*, XIII, 16).

Here, morality proceeds from the immediate to the remote, as in the Gospels; it takes the natural order of human feelings into account. But this is also because the family, like the city, is an autonomous system whose dependence does not conflict with its inner autonomy, based as both are on the feudal model.

There was also an occasion on which the governor of She questioned Tse-Lu about Confucius; here we have one of the best and perhaps as well one of the most touching descriptions of him. Tse-Lu did not know how to answer the question. Confucius said to him, "Yeu, why did you not answer? He is a man who seeks to achieve humanity (*jen*) with a zeal that causes him to forget to eat, who derives from this a joy that makes him forget his sorrows, and who does not see that old age is approaching" (*L.Y.*, VII, 18).

Some time thereafter Confucius went back to Ts'ai. Before he crossed a river, he sent Tse-Lu ahead to obtain information about the ford from two men who were working in a field. These men had been driven into seclusion by the troubles of the time, and they are known to us by the names of Ch'ang Ts'iu and Kie Ni. These names were coined by later annalists: *Ts'iu* means "he who does not emerge from his rest," and *Ni* means "he who remains at the bottom of the water and never rises." Ch'ang Ts'iu said to Tse-Lu: "Who is the man who is holding the reins in the chariot?"

"He is K'ong K'yu."

"K'ong K'yu of Lu?"

"Yes, that is he."

"Then," Ch'ang Ts'iu said, "he knows the ford."

It is rather difficult to determine whether this reply was spoken in malice or whether Ch'ang Ts'iu was implying that, journeying from one country to another as he did, Confucius

must have passed that way before. In any case, it was a veiled criticism of his attitude.

Tse-Lu then turned to Kie Ni, who asked, "Who are you?"

"I am Chong-Yeu."

"Are you not one of the disciples of K'ong K'yu of Lu?"

"Yes."

"The world is like a rushing torrent," Kie Ni said. "Who could change it? Rather than follow a wise man who flees human society, would it not be better to follow those who flee the whole world?"

Thereupon, the two men took up their harrow and began to cover the seed that they had sown.

Tse-Lu repeated the conversation to Confucius, who seemed to be grieved by it. "We cannot make the birds and the wild beasts our society," he said. "If I flee the company of men, with whom shall I live? If the world were well ordered, what need would I feel to want to change it?" (*L.Y.*, XVIII, 6).

During this same journey, Tse-Lu, who had lagged behind, lost sight of Confucius. Seeing an old man who was carrying on his shoulders a staff from which hung a basket in which to gather grass, Tse-Lu asked him whether he had seen the Master.

"Your four limbs have never felt the pain of labor," the old man answered. "You do not know how to tell the five kinds of cereal grain from one another. What is your master?" He added: "This is the season for working the fields. You depart on long journeys in your master's train. What does that profit the men of our time? Who even knows your master?"

Tse-Lu placed his hands together as a mark of respect. The old man invited him to spend the night in his house, killed a hen, prepared millet, and served a meal to his guest. Then he introduced his two sons.

The next day, when he had rejoined Confucius, Tse-Lu told him of the encounter. "Not to serve is not right," Confucius said. "If one cannot neglect the obligations due to age, how can one refuse those that exist between prince and subject? By trying

81

WITH THE HELP OF A STICK ON HIS SHOULDER
THE OLD MAN WAS CARRYING A BASKET IN WHICH TO GATHER GRASS

to keep oneself pure [of all compromise] one upsets the cardinal relation [of society]. The wise man serves according to the will of justice. That order does not prevail, we have long known" (*L.Y.*, XVIII, 7).

The shadow of failure was lengthening over his life. He was now sixty-three years old. In the course of his wanderings he had suffered the hostility of the powerful and the scorn of the wise. He thought of building a raft and floating down the river to the seas of the barbarians, or going to live among the nine barbarian tribes on the coast (*L.Y.*, V, 6; IX, 13). Nor did he

lack even a fool to provide the note of derision that human affairs merit; a fool, or a wise man who pretended madness in order to escape it and the troubles and the perils of the world. So the fool of Ch'u sang: "O phoenix! O phoenix! how your virtue decays! For the past, reproaches are vain; but for the future you can still be pursued. Stop! Stop! In today's times those who engage in politics see their lives in jeopardy" (*L.Y.*, XVIII, 5).

A short time later Confucius went back to Wei, which had always represented a mooring to him during his years of pilgrimage. Duke Ling had died shortly after Confucius had left the country. His grandson, Duke Chö, succeeded him only after having driven out his own father, who had tried to assassinate Princess Nan-tse, the grandmother of the one and the mother of the other. This state of affairs, in which, according to Confucius' morality, no one was where he belonged, in which the father did not behave as a father or the son as a son, in which the correctness of names was troubled, naturally offended Confucius. Although the young duke wanted him to become his counselor, undoubtedly in order to cloak himself in the sage's reputation, Confucius refused any appointment. For approximately six years he remained in obscurity, and there was no word of him.

RETURN TO LU

■ His disciple, Jen K'yu, who had entered the service of Ki Kang in Lu in 491 B.C., achieved a great military success against Ts'i in 483. The leader of the Ki clan asked him, "Are your military gifts innate or acquired through study?"

"I studied with Confucius," Jen K'yu replied.

"What sort of man is he?"

Jen K'yu's description of his teacher pleased Ki Kang. He wanted to summon Confucius to him, but he did not yet know whether Confucius would accept. "If you wish to summon him to you," Jen K'yu advised, "do not be narrow with him . . . then it will be feasible."

Ki Kang sent a messenger bearing gifts to Confucius, who returned to his native country in the eleventh year of the reign of Duke Ngai. He was then sixty-nine years old, and it was fourteen years since he had left his country in search of a prince.

Duke Ngai and Ki Kang honored him and occasionally asked his counsel, but in the end they did not appoint him to any office. It was true that his counsels were not such as could please the powerful men of the time, who sought to aggrandize themselves at any cost, even usurpation. For example, Confucius told Ki Kang that if the aristocrats were not covetous, their subordinates and the people would not steal, even if they were paid for so doing. He believed in the value of example, especially when it was handed down from above. "The virtue of the prince," he said, "is that of the wind; the virtue of the people is that of the grass. The grass bends in the direction of the wind" (*L.Y.*, XII, 17, 18).

So he spent his days in honor but also in unemployment, attending the duke's court regularly one day in every month, but only as a visitor. He systematized the classics inherited from the most remote past, which until then had been the subjects of study in his school: the *Shu king*, the *She king*, and a history of Lu, the *Ch'uen Ts'yu*. He attached great importance to this chronicle, in the expectation that posterity would judge him by it. He was also interested in the *Y king*, reading it so often that he wore out the thongs that bound the pages. He would have liked to live fifty years longer in order to study it. Did he write prefaces and commentaries for these works? It is possible, but not at all certain, at least as far as the *Y king* is concerned. He also brought order into music and the rites.

One day he noted that of all those who had been with him in his time of danger between Ch'en and Ts'ai, few still crossed his threshold. Some had accepted employment, others had departed from the world. In the same year in which he returned to Lu, he lost his favorite disciple, Yen Huei, who died prematurely. Confucius was deeply grieved. He mourned him for a long time and indeed excessively (*L.Y.*, XI, 8). Then his son, Pö-Yi, died in 482 B.C. Strangely, he accepted this loss with greater equanimity.

In the spring of 480 B.C. a coachman employed by Shu-suen captured a mysterious animal during a hunting party given by the duke. No one knew what it was, and Confucius was called in for consultation. He recognized it at once. It was the *k'i-lin*, the unicorn. Its left forefoot was lame, and its horn still bore the

IT WAS THE *k'i-lin* . . .

ribbon that his mother had placed on it. "Why has it come so late?" he cried. He covered his face with his hands and sobbed. "My doctrine is finished."

On this sentence the *Ch'uen Ts'yu* ends.

Late that year, news came to Lu that the Duke of Ts'i had been killed by one of his grand officers. This regicide filled Confucius with anger and outrage. Although he held no official position, he remembered that he was ranked immediately below a *tai-fu*. He fasted and bathed and solemnly presented himself at the duke's court, demanding that he act. The duke replied that

85

路水然請喪夫子如喪父而無服悔心喪三年

藥者則絰出則否喪畢門人治任將歸入揖于

子貢相向而哭各盡哀寔器懷子貢藥室墓

凡六年然後歸弟子及魯人從塚而家者

有餘室因命曰孔里

he was in no position to intervene in so powerful a country. "Half the people of Ts'i favor such intervention," Confucius said (*L.Y.*, XIV, 22). But the duke disclaimed responsibility and sent him to the head of the "three families."

In 479 B.C. Confucius learned of the death of the loyal Tse-Lu, who had faithfully stood by him in so many situations. Confucius had left him in Wei with Tse-Kao at the time of his own return to Lu. Both had accepted service with Wei. A revolution broke out, and the prudent Tse-Kao was able to flee. But Tse-Lu bravely threw himself into the battle. He fell beneath the walls of Ts'i-ch'eng, a place that still bears the same name today, and his grave can be seen there, five miles from K'ai-cheu, in southern Cheli (*L.Y.*, XI, 12). His body was cut to pieces and displayed at the eastern gate. Confucius had foretold this fate to Tse-Lu (*L.Y.*, XI, 12), nevertheless, he was deeply moved by it.

The next year, 478 B.C., two years after the appearance of the unicorn, Confucius rose early one morning. He walked before his door, trailing a staff, and he sang:

> *See how T'ai shan crumbles;*
> *How the great tree will be destroyed;*
> *And the wise man vanishes like a withered plant!*

At the sound of his song, Tse-Kong hurried to see how he was. "Why do you arrive so late, O Tse?" Confucius asked. Then he recounted a dream:

"Under the Hias, the coffin was placed at the head of the eastern stairway; under the Chus, at the head of the western stairway; under the Yins [Changs], between the two pillars. Last night I dreamed that I was sitting between the two pillars, facing the sacrifices that are made to the dead. No doubt this is because I am descended from the Yins [kings of Chang]."

He went back into the inner room to lie down. He never rose again: seven days later he died. It was the day of *ki-ch'u*, the

87

HE WAS BURIED ON THE BANK
OF THE SSEU RIVER

eleventh day of the fourth month of the sixteenth year of Duke
Ngai of Lu, or the forty-first year of the reign of King King of
Chu—478 B.C. He was in his seventy-third year.

Confucius was buried in the northern part of the capital of
K'iu-fu, on the shore of the Sseu River. Duke Ngai pronounced
the funeral oration: "Heaven has taken away the venerable man.
There is no one left to aid me. Alas! Woe is me! O venerable
Ni!"

His disciples "wore mourning in the heart"—that is, without
any visible token—for three years, as for a father. A hundred of
them even formed a settlement at his tomb. Tse-Kong remained
there for six years. (Today the tomb stands in the wood of
K'ong-lin amid thousand-year-old trees, in the village of K'ong-
li—both wood and village bear his name.) There, too, the duke
ordered the erection of a funeral temple, in which the relics of
the sage were brought together: his bonnet, his ceremonial vestments, his lute, and his chariot. And this was the beginning of
the cult of Confucius.

"When I had contemplated the hall of the funeral temple,"
Sseu-ma Ts'ien was to write in the second century B.C., "his
chariot, his vestments, his ritual utensils, all the masters who at
the prescribed times performed the rites in his dwelling, I tarried
there and could not depart. They are legion in this world who,
from sovereigns to wise men, have enjoyed in their lifetimes a
glory that ended with their lives. But the glory of Confucius,
though he was a man who wore linen, has been handed down
through more than ten generations. Those who devote themselves to study regard him as their patron. From the Son of
Heaven down, the kings and the lords, all who in the Middle
Kingdom discourse on the liberal arts guide themselves and
make their decisions according to the Master. That is what one
can call perfect sanctity" (*She ki*).

In 194 B.C. the founder of the imperial Han Dynasty went
there to pay homage. This was the consecration. And for more
than two thousand years, every dynasty emulated his example.

PORTRAIT

■ Confucius was tall, though his legs were rather short, if credence on the latter point is to be given to his school's Taoist adversary, Chuang-tse. He had the "five projections": protuberant eyes, a prominent nose with large nostrils, a pronounced Adam's apple, flat ears, and teeth that protruded slightly beyond his lips so that they were not quite closed. The bronze statue in the temple of Yushima Seido in Tokyo, which was supposed to have been brought there from K'iu-fu by a Chinese emigrant during the Ming period, very clearly shows two incisors jutting beyond the lips. His face was broad, with marks like those that are to be seen "on a ripe melon." His hands were strong, resembling a tiger's paws; his beard was luxuriant, his mouth was wide. His walk was rapid. His complexion was dark. It is difficult to determine whether this portrait is accurate. Nevertheless, with the exception of a few details, it is indeed the way in which he was pictured even by an adversary of the fourth century B.C. like Chuang-tse, who apparently regarded this description as a generally accepted fact. Marcel Granet, however, is skeptical, and views it as a conventionalized portrait of the sage; thus, the dark color is that of water and the symbol of depth.

His manner was gentle, calm, and austere; he inspired respect without arousing fear; he was sober and serene. When he was not busy, his appearance was cordial and gay (*L.Y.* VII, 4). In the presence of a man in mourning or a blind man, he rose. Mourning made it impossible for him to eat or sing. He was given to acts of spontaneous sensitivity. He was circumspect in his behavior. When he received on behalf of a prince, he kept his hands together, without moving his body, turned them to the right and to the left; in the same position, he raised his elbows like the wings of a bird when he was introducing guests. At court or in the temple he expressed himself clearly but with respectful attention and a noble gravity. With simple people he too was simple, though speaking little.

Chapter X of the *Luen yu* is devoted to what would obviously appear to us to be idiosyncrasies inspired by an ingenuous, complicated ritual symbolism. Even if questions were put to him, he never spoke while eating or in bed. He enjoyed drinking, but not to excess. He had a certain philosophy of dietetics, or food fads: he would eat nothing that had not been cut into equal portions; he always mixed a certain proportion of vegetables with his meat. When he was in a chariot, he always looked straight ahead, never turned backward, and never pointed to anything with his finger. He never wore clothes of certain shaded colors (for example, red tending toward blue); in other words, nothing that did not fall within the five clearly defined colors.

He paid great attention to everything that had to do with health, purifying abstinences, sacrifices, and military matters. He liked music and if someone sang a melody that pleased him, he would often ask to have it repeated. He was anything but a man who restricted himself to masochistic pleasures or mortifications.

On the other hand, it must not be thought that he was enslaved to excessive formalism. True, he was somewhat stiff. He was an advocate of balance and proportion in all things: "Courtesies that exceed the ritual norm are wearying. Circumspection beyond the ritual norm makes one fearful. Courage in excess of the ritual rule creates disorder" (*L.Y.*, VIII, 2).

He had a simple and accurate image of himself. It would be unjust to him to make him a superman. To be a man among men, a human being in a human society—and that is no small matter, as we can clearly see today—a society that is the heir of the civilizing work of the men of the past: this was all that he wished to be. But he devoted all his effort to it, with a view to being what he wished to be. He was not satisfied to evolve a doctrine or an ethical system. If he did so, it was in spite of himself and without his own knowledge.

"Meditation in order to understand, study and teaching without growing weary: are these not my merits?" (*L.Y.*, VII, 2).

90

至聖先師孔子
東兗州府曲阜縣人仲尼山

"Not applying myself to the achievement of virtue, not explaining clearly to myself what I study, not accomplishing what I conceive to be my duty, not correcting my own faults: these are my anxieties" (*L.Y.*, VII, 3).

He drew his knowledge from the men of the past: "I have no inborn knowledge. I love antiquity and I search for it assiduously" (*L.Y.*, VII, 19). And from the men of the present as well: "Among three men who are walking together (myself being one of them), I am certain to find my teacher, a good one in order to emulate him, and a bad one in order to [recognize in him what in myself I must] correct" (*L.Y.*, VII, 21).

He taught others with the same application and the same spirit: "Do I possess knowledge? No. But, when a man of humble condition questions me, even if he be stupid, I explain everything to him from beginning to end, omitting nothing" (*L.Y.*, IX, 7).

He knew the limitations of his efforts: "I dare not pretend to sanctity and perfect humanity. All that can be said of me is that I cultivate virtue without remission, that I teach without ever becoming discouraged" (*L.Y.*, VII, 33). There was nothing secretive about him: "My disciples, do you think that I am hiding something from you? I have done nothing of which you have been kept in ignorance" (*L.Y.*, VII, 23).

He had nothing of the esoteric. He avoided speaking of mysterious matters, such as miracles. He formulated no theories or universal maxims. He rarely discussed the fundamental virtue of *jen*—perfect humanity—undoubtedly because of the difficulty that he encountered in defining it. He spoke even less, or only to a few privileged persons, of the essence of man (*sing*) and the Way of Heaven. Nor did he talk of profit or acts of violence or disorders, lest he trouble men's hearts. At the same time he cherished in himself and in his bearing a feeling of reverence that seemed, according to the *Y king*, to be the precondition of inner order, a thoughtful, watchful sentiment that might be described as prayerful and that, as he said, made his life a prayer, something that found the source of its own transfiguration in being lived (*L.Y.*, VII, 34).

The surfaces of his portrait are in danger of being confused with those of his doctrine, and so I shall not pursue the catalogue of its characteristics. We see here, obviously, a humanism centered on concrete, practical observation, a humanism in both meanings of the word, in relation both to the past and to the present, in the undoubtedly poorly expressed sentiment of man's eternal present. "Become what you are," Goethe said. The Confucian maxim could be: "Become what man is." But what is man? That was the question posed by the Egyptian Sphinx that still lies at the border of our deserts.

夫
得
何
人
之
而
失
德
未
聖
屬
若
古
如
成
人
教
敢
古
天
大
礼

THE DOCTRINE

REACTION AND PROGRESS

■ In the biographical section we have considered Confucius in the society of his time. We have discussed his legitimism, important in the history of the Chinese consciousness, for "loyalty to the legitimate prince" was a fundamental of Chinese politics and ethics for more than two thousand years. It was a feudal element that gained a remarkable historical life span, and that it is desirable to understand in the context of its period.

The explanation of this legitimist attitude is easy. Confucius

95

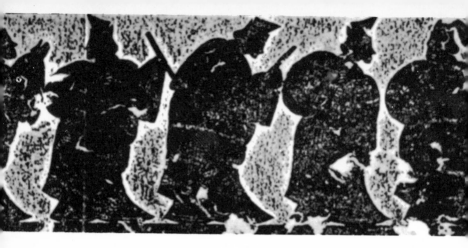

came from that circle of minor nobility whose position was extremely shaky and uncertain at the end of the period of *Ch'uen Ts'yu*. It was naturally oriented toward the weak, legitimate prince and against the oligarchy of the powerful noble clans of usurpers. These were the same reasons that caused the Third Estate in France to turn toward the king and against the aristocracy. Consequently, the Chinese nobles formed an idealized concept of the feudalism—courtly feudalism, as René Grousset called it—of the early centuries of the Chus, when the king assured order in the realm and actually reigned over the lords. Chivalry was similarly idealized in Europe. The true picture must have been quite different: their ideal represented a conservative utopia, or, more accurately, a reactionary utopia based on the past.

They did not, however, constitute a structured class, but rather a mixed class in the process of formation, born of a historical erosion that occurred somewhere in the social world, a historical nebula within which each man was alone and quaking in a measureless world. Younger sons of noble families, heirs of scribes, they were in the uncertain, ambiguous situation of the *discipuli vagabundi* of the European Middle Ages or the intellectuals of our own time. Their ethic could seek its sustenance and its significance only in the individual conscience; thus, it had a progressive tendency and marked an advance in conscience.

THE NOBLE AND THE MAGICIAN

■ Their ethic was aristocratic in spirit. It was that of the governing classes, or of those who aspired to become part of them. It was the ethic of the *kiun-tse*. This word is often translated, not incorrectly, as "wise man," but it is a translation of only half the meaning. The closest translation, in my opinion, would be "the princely man, the noble, the gentle man, the wise-gentle man" (*kiun*, "lord"; *tse*, "person," "thing," "son"). The word has undergone the same evolution as the word "noble" in French or English.

To be a *kiun-tse* meant to conduct oneself in conformity with the condition or calling of a ruling class. Whereas the schools for the children of the nobility had something of the military academy, the school of Confucius was a kind of academy of political science as conceived in the mind of Hippolyte Taine. The original aim is clearly apparent in this sentence: "The *kiun-tse* who studies wisdom loves mankind; the commonplace man (*siao jen*) who studies wisdom becomes easier to govern" (*L.Y.*, XVII, 4). Thus there was on the one hand he

97

THE GENTLEMAN
(HAN PERIOD)

who governed and on the other he who was governed.

But even the moral characteristics of the *kiun-tse* retained something of their social origin. Thus, he "is not an instrument" (*L.Y.*, II, 12). This means that he had no specialty, he was not a technician, he did not work on his own. His specialty was to view things from above, to govern. One is reminded of French secondary education, which prepares the student for nothing in particular and deals out "disinterested culture." The *kiun-tse* learned the art of speaking well from the *She king* and the art of governing from the *Shu king*. He studied the humanities. He practiced the rites in order to behave properly at court, in the temple, and in conferences among lords, and studied music for virtually the same reasons. Furthermore, he did not neglect shooting with the bow and driving the chariot— annual regattas were no more left out than at Oxford. All this attests to his military derivation. If, in addition, he was interested in the *Y king*, it was because the sciences of divination, or scapulomancy, and the calendar, or chronomancy, were part of the governmental function inasmuch as they were the sacerdotal (shamanist) heritage of the king-wizard, the clearer of the land, the master of irrigation, the rain-maker, charged with offering the sacrificial alcohol to the gods in the primitive agricultural communities. If he scorned profit and was ignorant of trade, artisanry, and other techniques, his reasons were the same as those of the Western nobleman. If he was poor, he preferred to cultivate his fields. His profession was to serve the state. "Not to serve is to be derelict in one's duty" (*L.Y.*, XVIII, 7, section 2).

Thus, he exerted influence by reason of the mere fact of his existence and his example. The *Chong Yong* (*The Golden Mean*) was to say: "By his mere movement the *kiun-tse* creates a path for the world; by acting he sets the rule for the generations; by speaking he offers the model for all. Those who are far off place their hope in him; those who are near do not weary of him" (*Ch.Y.*, 12, section 2).

Through the virtue that he has brought to reality in his person, the *kiun-tse* is like "a fixed polar star toward which all the other stars turn in a gesture of cosmic greeting" (*L.Y.*, II, 1). He acts as "silent" Heaven regulates the procession of the seasons. Here we find again the idea of "not acting," *wu-wei*, which had been thought to be peculiar to Taoism but which is shown to be a postulate common to all Chinese thought. On close inspection he is like the celebrant of a ceremonial who works in silence.

Thus we see a number of stages of history and even pre-history emerging in Confucius. We find the ideal of the noble-man of the court, the ideal of a military class, and the ideal of a priestly class. In India the two functions of the soldier and the priest are divided between the Brahmin and the *kchattrya*. Here they are indivisible: there is communication between them.

Nature finds the model for the dualism of *yin* and *yang* in the social morphology of the primitive communities. This reflects

PI, SYMBOL OF HEAVEN   TSONG, SYMBOL OF EARTH
(CHU PERIOD, AGE OF THE FIGHTING KINGDOMS)

the organization of labor into two competing, united guilds: the women who weave and the men who till the soil. The two groups lived separately and met only in the orgiastic festivals of spring and autumn. But the social order, on the other hand, was indebted to the life of nature, the worship of nature, for its mystery and its profundity, for what gave it its metaphysical dimension.

Because of its historic and prehistoric roots, then, the ethic of the *kiun-tse* has a clearly political character. In the *Li Ki* (*Notes* on *Rites*), Confucius is quoted as saying, "Politics is the great matter in the life of men." One is reminded of the axiom attributed to Napoleon: "Politics is the destiny of nations." But here the word has a double connotation: a political meaning and a metaphysical or religious meaning.

This is true of the entire Confucian terminology, which on that account is resistant to translation. Thus the rites represent court etiquette and at the same time religious ritual, which is infused with the spirit of primitive magic. Similarly, the

101

word that we translate as "sanctity" (*cheng*) alludes not only to inner accomplishment but also to a kind of outer—super-natural—power over men and things. The books speak of the "holy kings," who preserve the order not only of society but also of the universe, for the two do not form two separate realms. Their work "is the equal of that of Heaven and Earth." The *K'ong-tse Si-yu* was to say of the "realized man":

> The virtue [*heng*] of the realized man consists in under-standing the reason of the heart [literally: the nature of man and of his feelings], the secret of the transformation of things, the cause of what is mysterious and holy, in penetrating to the source of the wandering principle [the spiritual principle which runs through life and death]. Only then is a man realized. Thus one knows the Way of Heaven and then in one's life one practices the virtue of perfect humanity [*jen*] and the duty of justice in interpersonal relations [*yi*]; one embellishes oneself with the rites and with music. Humanity, justice, the rites, and music: these are [what constitute] the virtue [*heng*] of the realized man, the knowledge of the spiritual principle of transformations: that is what defines his fruitful power [*tö*].*

The text is rather obscure. *Heng* and *tö*, words that are often coupled together to form a single concept, are used indifferently, one in place of the other, in contradictory meanings. This confusion, however, shows that the idea of virtue has a dual meaning, a magic as well as a moral signification. This relation between moral realization and power is obvious in all the incarnations of Chinese thought. (It is not wholly alien to Catholicism.) The inter-penetration of the two terms—and the second is the stronger—has been felicitously summed up by Fong Yeu-Lan in this phrase: "wisdom within and royalty without."

---

* Quoted by Tran TrongKim in *Nho-giao*, volume I, page 173.

It has been said that the Roman Church proceeds not by mutations but by accumulations of truths. In analogous fashion, Chinese thought maintains a certain continuity among the various strata of historical experience. It is rooted; that is the reason for China's profound balance. Throughout all her intellectual life there persists something of that indivisibility of her original society and soul that prevailed before the separation of social functions came as the prelude to the separation in intellectual operations. In this she has been aided by her language. That primitive stratum seems to have provided the metaphysical tonality for her thought. Indeed, perhaps all metaphysics is only the resurgence in us, as a memory or a nostalgia, of that original indivisibility at the root of our fragmented, departmentalized, rationalized, and also rationed life.

THE TIME OF HEROES

■ This unitary view of reality comes naturally into opposition to the spirit of analysis, to the spirit of system, and, if one may say so, to government by system. It appeals to the individual. It favors the hero. The eagle that guards its solitude on the rock in Chinese paintings is the image of the hero, the hero from the marches who goes forth to conquer a kingdom among the barbarians. He is the dragon with the unpredictable moves that the *Y king* shows us, first hidden and invisible beneath the waters (the hidden wise men) and then "appearing in the plain" when "the time" has come—not a static term but a living time that nurtures a meaning and a cipher, that contains opportunities, that reveals abrupt mutations. It is a time of heroes, and "the cold of winter" constitutes the test and the proof of "the pines and the cypresses" (*L.Y.*, IX, 26). Centuries can go by during which they are not seen and the world is abandoned to disorder.

"The policy of Kings Wen and Wu is set forth in the ancient books; if men like them exist, that policy is put into practice; if they disappear, that policy disappears with them" (*Ch.Y.*, 20).

THE HUMANITY OF MAN

■ The Confucians, if not Confucius, have drawn up the catalogue of moral obligations: *jen* (perfect humanity), *yi* (equity), *li* (protocol and ritual), *che* (perspicacity, intelligence), and *sin* (good faith, fidelity to the pledged word).

Is this order logical? Probably not. It may have been a mnemonic technique governed by the harmony of the sounds in the Chinese language. It is somewhat reminiscent of the list of the theological virtues. Sometimes it is given with only four items, which are then made to correspond to the four "categories" of the *Y king*: the second virtue, for example, which is so difficult to define and translate, corresponds to the idea of a redistribution of wealth, the third to a concept of esthetics.

The translation of the first two terms, *jen* and *yi*, is unquestionably rough. When Couvreur translated *jen* to mean "perfect virtue," he drowned its reality in the void. Of necessity, any word that refers to a broad sentiment of many interpretations has a specific meaning only in a specific context. That is why Plato's Eros is not identical with Christian love. To us "charity" has a Christian connotation, but it does not necessarily mean this, and it has not always done so. There can be no doubt that *jen* relates to a sentiment of this nature, but in order to avoid connecting it with Christianity it is translated either in vague terms or in others that specialize its meaning and restrict its application: for example, "beneficence." I believe that it desig-

104

nates simply human and interpersonal feeling, humanity in its fullness and its excellence.

Although he had asserted that his doctrine was governed by a single principle (*L.Y.*, XV, 2), Confucius avoided general questions. He was concerned above all with what was concrete and practical. Probably, too, this was because the Chinese language, which rebels at concepts, does not encourage definitions. He did not like to discuss *jen*. Furthermore, what he said of it differed according to who recorded his words. But on more than one occasion, I think, he was sufficiently explicit.

" 'Is there one precept,' Tse-Kong asked him, 'that can guide action throughout life?'

" 'Love,' Confucius answered. 'Not to do to others what one does not wish done to oneself' " (*L.Y.*, XV, 23).

This is the precept of the Gospels. To Fan Ch'e he gave a short answer: "Love mankind" (*L.Y.*, XII, 21). To his question on knowledge, he replied in the same dialogue: "Know mankind." But the political character of his thought lay in the fact that for him this knowledge had a purpose: the selection of men suited to the functions of government. During this same walk with Fan Ch'e at the foot of the hill of Wu-yu, he was to insist on the practical realization of *jen* in one's person and above all in one's actions (*L.Y.*, XII, 20). And to Yen-Huei he said, "To observe oneself and correct oneself, to obey the rites: that is *jen.*"

Later he told Chong-Kong, "When one goes out, one should conduct oneself as if one were receiving a distinguished guest; with respect to the people one should behave as if one were celebrating solemn sacrifices; what one does not wish done to oneself one should not do to others" (*L.Y.*, XII, 2).

This meant the interdiction of negligence, slovenliness, and excessive familiarity, and the emphasis on the feeling of the gravity and solemnity of human obligation in great matters and small. Elsewhere he said to Tse-Chang, "*Jen* is the capacity to accomplish five things in the world, namely: self-respect,

106

magnanimity, good faith and loyalty, diligence, and beneficence . . . Then one can command others" (*L.Y.*, XVII, 6).

He compared the nature of *jen* with that of a mountain, which is self-contained in its serenity and its tranquility. Although such comparisons were somewhat rash, one cannot help thinking of those verses in the Biblical Psalms in which God is likened to a rock. Confucius said: "How high is the mountain! How high it is! How I love it! Vegetation thrives on it; birds and animals live on it; it contains riches in abundance. The wealth belongs to all. Everyone can go and seek it. The wind and the clouds go forth from there to establish communication between heaven and earth, the harmonious union between *yin* and *yang*."

But *jen* can also be defined by its opposite: Chinese medicine likens paralysis to the lack of *jen*—in other words, to a state of insensitivity. *Jen* is so natural that "it is not far off; he who seeks it has already found it" (*L.Y.*, VII, 29). It is close to man and never leaves him.

It would appear, however, that some restriction was envisaged for this virtue of humanity, this imitation distinguished it from sanctity (*cheng*). Tse-Kong inquired of the Master: "To distribute one's benefactions to the whole people and help everyone without exception—is that *jen?*"

"Is it indeed *jen?*" Confucius asked. "Is it not, rather, sanctity? [Kings] Yao and Shuen themselves knew the grief of not attaining to it. The man who has *jen* stands firm and strengthens others; he succeeds and he makes others succeed. On the basis of what is near he judges what is proper for the remote" (*L.Y.*, VI, 28).

This limitation of *jen* found concrete expression in at least one instance. Confucius was asked, "What is your opinion of returning good for evil?"

He replied, "Then what would you return for good? Evil must be returned with rectitude, good with good [more precisely: virtue with virtue]" (*L.Y.*, XIV, 36).

Here we are a long way from the principle of the Gospels.

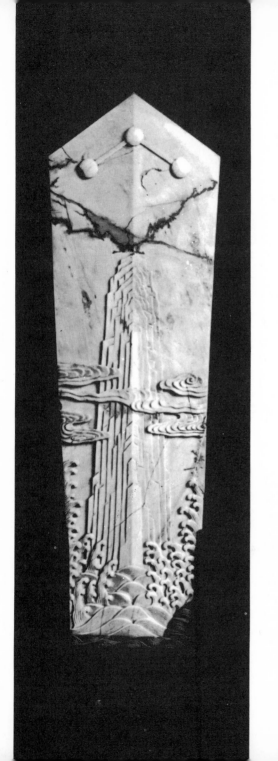

THE MOUNTAIN THAT
REMAINS AT REST
(JADE OF THE T'ANG PERIOD)

We are also far from the "universal love" that was to be preached by Mö-tse (or Mö Ti) something less than a century later. Not only is there no question of offering the other cheek: one ought not to allow oneself to be gulled. But that must not cause one to lose the faith in mankind that one ought to have. "He is truly wise who, without assuming in advance that others are endeavoring to deceive him or that they distrust him, is capable of penetrating deceptions at the proper time" (*L.Y.*, XIV, 33).

And whence does he derive this remarkable power? Is this an instance of counseling practical psychology? For, as is well known, trust begets trust and distrust begets distrust. Or does prudence find the secret of its strength in the virtue of the soul?

Love here is differentiated love, a kind of distributive justice, dealing out *jen*, which goes undoubtedly from the near to the far, which distinguishes between what is you and what is I, as Granet observed, and not only yours and mine but also what seems to assume its proportion and its rule in the context of the social order. In this society there are fundamental relationships: the relation between prince and subject, on which all the others seem to be formulated, the relation between teacher and disciple, between father and son, between husband and wife (*Ch.Y.*, 20, section 3). *Yi*, which is often inadequately translated as "duty, equity, justice," means the distributive justice of *jen* within a system of interpersonal relations. Thus, there would be the *yi* as between prince and subject, as well as the *yi* of timely action—that is, accorded to *time* in a chronomantic sense.

In the achievement of *jen* there are, so to speak, virtues that are means, as *jen* is a basic virtue, although the distinction is not altogether certain. Thus *sin*, good faith and loyalty to the pledged word—the last of the five virtues—has been compared with a piece of harness that is essential to the whole and without which the team cannot be driven (*L.Y.*, II, 22). The same is true of courage (*yung*); prudence (*che*), almost in the sense of the Christian theological virtue; and sincerity (*ch'eng*), according to the *Chong Yong* (20, section 3).

In a diverting illustration of this last, *ch'eng* is clearly compared with a base for paint. Tse-Hia said to Confucius, "A pleasant smile elegantly models the corners of the mouth; the beautiful eyes shine with black and white splendor. A blank base receives divers colors.* What is the meaning of these words?"

"Before one can paint," Confucius replied, "one must have a blank background. Therefore this means that ritual presupposes sincerity of feeling" (*L.Y.*, III, 8).†

But it would remain for the Master's grandson to exalt sincerity: "Sincerity is the beginning and end of all things . . ." (*Ch. Y.*, 25). "It is only the man who possesses complete sincerity . . . who will wholly develop his nature. Wholly developing his own nature, he will also develop those of others. Developing those of others, he will also develop the natures of animals and things. Developing the natures of beings and things, he takes part in the work of transformation and life of Heaven and Earth" (*Ch.Y.*, 22). Sincerity in fact becomes, in one lyric movement, the virtue of Heaven and Earth. It functions as a magic influence.

Ritual and music—although ritual had acquired such importance that it had become almost an end—are also in the category of means. They are the outward manifestations of the "single principle" on the plane of the multiplicity of human action. Tse-Kong, who was reputed to be elegant as well as eloquent—and this was not unimportant in the Confucian scheme —tells us, "One must look after the external as well as the internal. If the hair is stripped from it, the skin of a tiger or a leopard cannot be distinguished from the skin of a dog or a sheep" (*L.Y.*, XII, 8).

---

* A quotation from *The Odes*.

† The anecdote shows, incidentally, that as early as the time of the *She king* (eighth century B.C.) women painted their eyes with black as they do today and as we know that they did in the Han period.

The outward influences the inward, and the behavior of a man who wears mourning is not the same as that of one who wears court dress or military armor. As *jen* is the substance of ritual, so ritual is "the reality of *yi*." "The influence of ritual in the shaping of man is secret; it forestalls evil before it can appear; it brings good nearer and thrusts evil away in an imperceptible fashion without our awareness of it" (*Li Ki*, chapter on *King kiai*).

The difference between music and ritual is that ritual differentiates and music unites or harmonizes; music impels to intimacy, friendship, union, the growth of emotions, while ritual fosters mutual respect and distance. They play complementary parts in the preservation of both the psychic and the social orders.

Hence, the humanity of *jen* is not an abstract humanity or a Platonic archetype, or something that is governed from a heaven that is inaccessible to consciousness in the splendor of its solitude and the uniqueness of its experience. It is the feeling of man's reality and his state among men. It is in society, in the embrace of civilization, that man's humanity fulfills itself. Confucius tells us of his pleasure in going to bathe with others at the source of the Y, in singing in chorus, in studying in a group. "Is it not a pleasure to study regularly? Is it not a pleasure to welcome friends who come from afar [to study together]?" (*L.Y.*, I, 1).

LADIES DRESSING

He counseled his disciples to have friends and companions, to nurture the spirit of concord, to be open to all, but not to be partisan. He believed in human perfectibility. He made no distinctions among the categories of men (*L.Y.*, XV, 38) and, since the word *lei*, used here in the sense of "category," can also mean "race," it would hardly be anticipating to say, as Tran Trong-Kim did, that he was anti-racist. In his school he accepted pupils from a village who were supposed to be incapable of learning. At times he spoke of going to preach his doctrine among the barbarians. He believed in human brotherhood. When poor Sseu-ma Niu (who was also rich and brave) complained, "Everyone has brothers. I am the only one who has none," he was answered in Confucius' school: "Within the four seas all men are brothers" (*L.Y.*, XII, 5).

In no case could there be any other way for mankind. "Who can go out otherwise than through the door? Who can walk otherwise than along his road?" (*L.Y.*, VI, 15).

Like certain passages of the Old Testament, this hushed anticipation of the future "I am the way and life and truth" is

112

charged for us with a sentiment of prophecy. But what then is that path for man, *jen tao*, what accomplishments does it demand of us, and, finally, if one studies, what does one study? For there is no signpost to a categorical imperative or a divine commandment to be seen along that path. Here, undoubtedly fragmentary and reminiscent of the wreckage of a tumbled monument, the texts are hardly explicit, and it is as if they were dealing with something understood in advance. But we have the right to know what that something understood is. It seems probable that it consists in respect for the cardinal or basic rules of society (and of course Confucius could conceive of no society other than the one that he knew and on the basis of which alone he was able to "idealize"); respect for the gods of the city (the gods of the soil and the harvest), though keeping them at something of a distance; all with a view to finally assuring peace and order, the preservation and the lives of men, animals, and things, their production and reproduction. It is in this modest endeavor, great in its political significance, that the *kiun-tse* becomes the equal of Heaven and Earth from the

LUTE (PERIOD OF THE FIGHTING KINGDOMS)

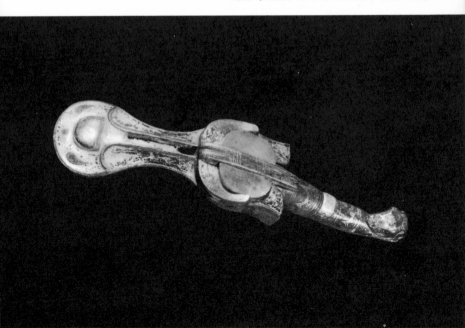

point of view of a universalist mysticism. And it is with this function in view that he is educated. Clearly establishing the parallelism, somewhat like Aristotle, the *Chong Yong* tells us, "The activity of man is politics; the activity of the earth is the production of vegetation" (*Ch.Y.*, 20).

ET NUNC, REGES TERRAE . . .

■ A compendium of advice and counsel to a prince could be drawn from Confucius, but this would not make him a Machiavelli. We are so accustomed to viewing the Italian as a master of political realism that we cannot imagine other forms of this political realism. We are closer to Confucian truth when we remember the *Et nunc, erudimini . . .* that Bossuet threw in the Sun King's face.

"The danger," the *Hi-tse* says, "lies in believing that one is secure on the throne and can enjoy it; loss comes from being too certain of possession; trouble arises out of believing that everything is in order. Therefore in time of peace the *kiun-tse* thinks of the hour of peril . . ."

He must be foresighted and vigilant, for "Heaven loves no one especially; it sustains him who is virtuous; the heart of the people is changeable; it loves him who regales it with favors. Not everyone does good works in the same fashion, but the result is peace and order. Not everyone does evil in the same fashion, but the result is disorder" (*Shu king*).

Punishment, as we see, is immediate. Confucius offered a definition of politics that runs counter to the practice of the modern politician. Playing on a homonym, he asserted, "Politics [*cheng*] is rectitude [*cheng*]" (*L.Y.*, XII, 16).

The famous theory of the "rectification of names" meant first of all harmony between what one says and what one does. "If

114

one is upright, one has no need to give orders in order to be listened to. If one is not, it is useless to give orders, because one will not be followed" (*L.Y.*, XIII, 6). By his virtuous example the *kiun-tse*, the princely man, must be to the people like "the polar star that remains fixed in its place" (*L.Y.*, II, 1). Otherwise, the people does not know "where to put its hands and feet," or, in modern parlance, what road to take. The law inscribed on bronze (this procedure had begun to be adopted in Cheng shortly before the time of Confucius) could undoubtedly fulfill this function. But, in addition to the fact that it encouraged the spirit of litigation, it did not make the people ashamed of doing wrong (*L.Y.*, II, 3), for obviously supervision could not be maintained everywhere, and the collaboration of the people with the government was essential. What the people were required to do ought to be clear and simple, and the government ought to begin by setting the example first (*L.Y.*, XIII, 1). One must begin by toiling without ever allowing oneself to be stopped by weariness before one could appeal to one's underlings. What was to be done after that? Reversing Guizot's observation, "Enrich yourselves," Confucius would say, "Enrich the people." And then? Educate it, and at all costs win its confidence. If among the three things that constitute a nation's strength—the economy, the army, and the people's confidence—any is to be sacrificed, it is better to give up the first two. But to lose the third would be fatal (*L.Y.*, XII, 7). Justice and even equality must be guaranteed.

"The prince should be afraid not of having a small population but of not having a [just] distribution of wealth. He ought to be afraid not of being poor but of not being in harmony" (*L.Y.*, XVI, 1, section 3).

It would probably be impossible to speak without anachronism, as Creel has done, of the democratic spirit of Confucianism. Nevertheless, it is not inappropriate to speak of a certain love for the people in connection with it. For the people was not altogether without defense. In contrast to the baron of medieval

115

Europe, the lord in Chinese antiquity was not too well protected by his armor, which in the beginning was made of rhinoceros skin, the stiffness of which prevented him even from saluting; later it was composed of layers of leather laid on like scales. The people could flee from one state to take up residence in another. The fear of not having a large population was often expressed, for the population could determine the issue of a battle by deserting, as has happened in China in recent years.

That is why the Chinese equivalent of *vox populi, vox Dei* recurs constantly in the *Shu king* from the earliest ages. "Heaven has compassion for the people; what the people desires, Heaven does" (Part I, Chapter I, 7). "Heaven sees through the eyes of my people and hears through the ears of my people" (Part IV, Chapter I, 7).

THE GOLDEN MEAN AND
THE FITTING MEDIUM

■ King Yao is supposed to have said to his successor, the legendary Shuen, "Well, Shuen, the time set by Heaven for your accession to the throne has come. Observe the mean [*chong*] in all things" (*L.Y.*, XX, 1). Confucius offered us some idea of what that mean was: "I know why the way is not followed: the intelligent man goes beyond it, the imbecile does not go far enough" (*Ch.Y.*, 4).

Hence our golden or just mean. No excess. No prejudgment. No saying in advance: "This is possible, that is impossible." In short, a wise opportunism coupled with a wise empiricism. But no doubt the meaning of these precepts must be sought beyond them, through investigation of pre- and post-Confucian texts. I shall justify the method.

116

The idea of a mean—a just mean—refers to a state of balance and harmony in a soul firmly established in its justice and its rightness. It has not yet been troubled by the disordered currents of sensibility, the "seven sentiments": joy, anger, sadness, etc. Sincerity reveals it in its purity and unity.

"The heart of man is unstable; the heart of wisdom is subtle; only through its purity and unity can one maintain oneself at the mean" (*Shu king*, Part I, Chapter III, 15). This state of the soul is the state of knowledge at its best: "without thought, without action, silent, without movement, moved, it penetrates the reason of the universe." By this is meant a perception by the soul, which can function only under certain conditions. This is the "natural light" of which the *Ta Hio* (*The Great Study*) speaks; indeed, it demands a certain freedom for the soul with respect to thought. Thus, a subtle distinction between soul and thought is to be observed here, a distinction that was noted also by St. Augustine. It is well known that in Buddhism what we call "consciousness" is precisely nescience, ignorance, the product of our relations with the illusory world of phenomena, concealing from us, as by an invisible veil, the transphenomenal Reality. But Chinese thought is more strongly characterized by a practical and political concern.

"Dwelling on the same thought enables you to be understood and followed by only a few," the *Y king* says. One must create a vacuum in one's soul, and the method is known to all mystics.

"I should like to speak no more," Confucius said to his disciples.

"If you did not speak," Tse-Kong countered, "what teachings could your disciples transmit?"

"Does Heaven speak? And yet the four seasons follow their courses and all beings grow" (*L.Y.*, XVII, 18).

Knowledge and action are silent. It is futile and harmful to indulge oneself in doctrinal disputes and attack opposing doctrines (*L.Y.*, II, 16), for there is a state of harmony in which "the ten thousand beings grow and reproduce without harming one another, and contradictory doctrines are practiced without conflict with one another, in which the minor virtues flow like brooks and the great virtues develop and transform [beings and things]" (*Ch.Y.*, 30, section 2). "Why does the world create cares for itself? All roads lead to the same place. All thoughts go to the same conclusion. Why does the world create cares for itself?" (*Hi-tse*).

This is a description of an Eden-like state of the soul, the mind, and the world, through which China is allied with the old nostalgia of all mankind and shares in the same anticipation. The soul is in accord and communication with the world. And the pacified human and natural worlds pursue the same destiny under the shepherd's crook of a "holy king," in whom it is easy to identify the figure of the primitive wizard. But this Eden is transported into the domain of knowledge, action, politics, and morality.

In this state in which we are at the center, at the "golden mean" (the original meaning of the character *chong* was "pivot"), the meaning of time and of becoming, and, as Lanza del Vasto would say, the "cipher of things," is revealed to us, and we can engage in timely and fitting action. Here one can recognize a notion that very obviously derives from the spirit of divination. The magician is also a seer and, like the prophets, he knows the future. Time here is meant in the chronomantic sense of divination. It is not a passive environment, but one of activity and liturgy. The process of becoming that takes place in it is transformation, mutation, gradation, flow, and, perhaps, eternal return. "When it has reached the end of itself, it is transformed; transformed, it flows; flowing, it endures." And enduring is living. The meaning of the universal becoming is the production of life.

All this must be seen in that rather mysterious remark by Confucius in which he seems to arrive at the Taoist idea of "not acting," *wu-wei*: "Not acting and making order prevail: that is what Shuen did. And how did he do it? He was constantly reverent and he kept his face turned toward the south; that is all" (*L.Y.*, XV, 4). Here there is every ground to talk of a magic consciousness.

This state is in no way static: it represents a conquest; it requires a great spiritual strength. "Heaven's action is powerful. The *kiun-tse* should always be strong." A perpetual effort of adaption and renewal is required of him. "To renew oneself every day and still to renew oneself every day" is a maxim that was carved on King T'ang's bath. We encounter even a paraphrase of the Gospels: "When Heaven created beings, it gave to each according to his character; it gave more to him who already had, and it overthrew him who was tottering" (*Ch.Y.*, 17, section 2).

On the whole it was a morality of will power. "A general can be deprived of his army, but a man cannot be deprived of his will" (*L.Y.*, IX, 24).*

---

* In analyzing the concept of the "mean" (*chong*) I have used some pre- and some post-Confucian writings, on the one hand, the *Chong Yong*, a work ascribed to the grandson of Confucius, and on the other hand, a collection of historical documents, the *Shu king*, and a book of divination, the *Y king*, especially its appendix entitled *Hi-tse*. The *Shu king* was taught in the school of Confucius, and it is completely legitimate to resort to it in quest of some reflection of the Master's thought. The *Y king* occupied his attention in the final period of his life; he had read it so many times that he had broken the thongs that held together the boards of wood or bamboo of which the book was made. But it is the sections of commentary, the appendices (called "wings"), that are the most interesting. They are attributed to Confucius, but this attribution is strongly challenged by informed critics. The general thesis is that the ideas expounded in these appendices belonged to the fourth century B.C. and that the work has experienced numerous interpolations at the hands of scholars and forgers during the last two centuries B.C., at the beginning of the Han Dynasty, the period when work was beginning on the reconstruction of the books burned in the proscription of 213 B.C. But this is a general thesis; it is difficult to prove it in detail and, what is more, it applies to all books of the period. Thus, the discovery of bronze Chu vases dating from the early centuries of the first millennium B.C. and bearing inscrip-

tions has made it possible to draw comparisons of style and language that tend to show that only a quarter of the *Shu king* is genuine. Nevertheless, the quotations that I have taken from the *Luen yu* (*The Conversations*), certainly the most reliable of the texts (though not entirely reliable), show that there is no contradiction between the thought that is implicit or in embryo in that work and the thought that is more or less—though hardly more—explicit in the others. It would be ill-advised to overlook the fact that the *Luen yu* is a collection of notes by students, extremely brief and radically condensed, in which facts and ideas are just barely indicated. In addition, out of practical concern for his teaching, Confucius avoided dealing with questions that were too general, and he did not readily reveal his thought on "the nature of man and the Way of Heaven." But that in no sense means that he never spoke of these things. In reality, to the extent to which it is valid, an internal criticism of the texts indicates that we have here a common fund of thought, an "institutional fund," as Granet called it, that led quite naturally, beginning even before Confucius, from primitive magic to metaphysical speculation.

THE *Luen Yu* CARVED IN STONE
(NINTH CENTURY A.D.)

CHARM TO
ROUT DEMONS

MAGIC CONSCIOUSNESS

■ What constitutes this magic consciousness that we have mentioned? Magic is action. But it does not travel the long road of causal mechanism. Like science, it proposes to act on nature. Thus, it has been possible to conclude that Bacon's reflections on magic opened the way to science. But causality in magic is modeled on our inner, or psychological, causality. We speak a word, the key word, the magic word, a word of command, and people obey us. Primitive man extended these two types of causality to the whole of nature. They were not the only types that he knew, for his real action on things, though limited, was in no way different from ours. But he went farther in emotion. He surcharged his real action with action of an oral and psychological kind, the word being the best imitation of action. Hence, he saw psychologies in all nature, and finally he saw

122

one single psychology and emerged into pan-psychism. This is the source of the Chinese theory of the unity of the universe, and perhaps even that pursued by Einstein was not radically different: it is quite as rational to imagine the world as pure chaos. It is a question of a mystic universe, a universe of soul, action, and will, the undivided universe of the original soul.

This universe, all tinged with magic, has the invincible mystery of the landscapes intersected by mist and invaded by dream that we see in Chinese painting. It began in chaos. At the heart of this chaos was the *T'ai ki* (the Great Pinnacle), of whom the priest-king, the agricultural prince, seems to have been the visible incarnation. He held his scepter as he would have held the pivot of the world. The three concepts of pinnacle, pivot, and mean seem to merge. From this Great Pinnacle, which was also called the Great Unity, came the two regulators, *yin* and *yang,* and the four cardinal points, the infinite combinations of which created the whole process of becoming. In the beginning, these two essential "categories" of the classification of things —forces or principles, it is not known which—were symbolized by designating the sunlit and the shaded sides of a mountain. Becoming the principles for the explanation of natural processes, they came in the end to designate the female and the male, the odd and the even, the cold and the hot, the soft and the hard, etc., laying the foundation for a universal dualism.

The world is becoming and change, transformations, gradations. "It flows night and day and never rests," Confucius, speaking like Heraclitus, said when he looked at a river. The world is likened to a door that "sometimes opens and sometimes closes," alternately. "It has no dwelling," the *Hi-tse* says; "it travels through the six voids [regions]; sometimes above, sometimes below; sometimes hard, sometimes soft; no rule can be found in it; only change is proper to it." What comes to the end of itself is transformed—defeat, for example, into victory, supremacy into decline—following a cyclical law. Within the mystery of transformations and mutations there is always the movement of a universal principle, that "wandering spirit" (*yeu k'i*), a vagabond spirit that journeys through life and death. If one learns the secret of these transformations, one knows the actions of the gods. And only the saint knows them, established in the center of himself as if at the center of the universe, like King Shuen, his solemn face turned toward the south. To him the meaning of time was made known. Its silent influence, hidden and beneficent, extends over things and beings. The lyrical *Chong Yong* tells us of its grandeur, its unity, and its simplicity:

"The path of wisdom is broad and secret. Ignorant men and women can know it; but thorough knowledge of it is not attained even by the saint; men and women without talent can practice it; but thorough practice of it is not attained even by the saint" (*Ch.Y.*, 12). Or again: "The doctrine of the wise man fastens itself in the hearts of the simple, but in the end it reaches to Heaven and Earth" (*Ch.Y.*, 12, section 2).

GOD AND THE GODS

■ Confucius—at least in the *Luen yu*—did not willingly deal with matters that did not have a practical aspect. He spoke of them only in an implicit manner. When Tse-Lu questioned him about death, he replied, "You do not know what life is; how could you know what death is?" During the same conversation, Tse-Lu asked him how one must serve the spirits and the gods, and Confucius answered, "You do not know how to serve men. How could you serve the gods?" (*L.Y.*, XI, 11).

His counsel was to "respect them but keep one's distance from them" (*L.Y.*, VI, 20). Perhaps he was speaking of a time when, as the result of barbarian influences, every house had its own god and its own priest (a sorcerer or magician), and the gods lived among men in complete equality. The ancient kings, *She king* tell us, ordered these practices abolished, reserving worship to the Son of Heaven and his appointees. Confucius recommended that sacrifices be offered to the gods as if they were in fact present (*L.Y.*, III, 12). What was essential in his eyes lay elsewhere: "He who offends against Heaven [through wrongful conduct] gains nothing by making sacrifices" (*L.Y.*, III, 13).

He said of his own life that it was a continuing prayer. He preferred to admit his ignorance of sacrifices to God himself, Ti, the Lord of Heaven, the Primordial Ancestor: "I do not know. Anyone who did know would have no more difficulty in governing the world than in turning his hand" (*L.Y.*, III, 10). And he made the gesture.

To him this was sacred ground. He felt that he had no more right to discuss it than a Catholic would claim to make pronouncements on articles of faith. He must have simply shared the beliefs of his time, inherited from the past and clarified by the holy kings. Otherwise, he spoke quite often of Heaven, the gods, and the spirits, but in an allusive manner, as of things already understood. Gods and spirits existed in unbelievable number: tutelary gods of the home, the soil, the road, the mountains and rivers, the harvest, etc., and of course the ancestral spirits. As for the rites of the various cults, we know how much importance Confucius ascribed to them.

There are irrefutable proofs of the Chinese belief in God in the *She king*, the most reliable and the oldest of the pre-Confucian texts. "Great is the Lord on high . . . He scrutinizes the four corners of the world, seeking someone who can establish his people. The first two Dynasties were incapable of satisfying him. Therefore he seeks in all the principalities the man to whom he can entrust power" (*She king*, III, i, 7). "The puissant wrath of unfathomable Heaven is felt everywhere in the world" (*She king*, II, v, 7).

God is "veiled in obscurity" (*She king*, II, v, 4; II, iv, 10;

125

quoted by Suzuki). One is reminded of what was written by
the unknown author of *The Cloud of Ignorance*, a fourteenth-
century English mystic of the school of St. Victor: it is quite
obviously our *Deus absconditus*. A poem of Kia Yi (198–166
B.C.), which I translated some time ago in Yggdrasill, employs
the same image that was used by the English mystic:

> *Beneath the pine I question the child.*
> *The Master has gone to gather herbs.*
> *He points him out to me in the distant mountain.*

126

Through the deep clouds I cannot see the place.

It would be impossible not to recognize in this some of the familiar themes of Christian mysticism: the child who is the gateway to knowledge; the remedy for the cure of the world; the "cloud of ignorance."

God "has neither sound nor scent" (*She king*, II, iv, 8; III, iii, 10; III, i, 1). This is a theme repeated often in the *Chong Yong*, which has plumbed it in depth, broadened it, yet not really explicited it. "The three kings are in Heaven," *The Odes* tell us again. Or: "King Wen moves to the right and the left of the Lord [Ti]." In the *Shu king* we see that early in his life Shuen lived near Mount Li.

"He went into the fields every day to cry out to compassionate Heaven and his parents, taking all the guilt on himself and charging himself with their wickedness" (Part I, Chapter III, 21). Or again: "There are no offerings that the spiritual beings always accept; they accept only those that are made with a sincere heart."

But the *Li Ki* provides us with an interesting clarification: "[The ceremony of] *kiao* in honor of Heu T'si [the mythical ancestor of the kings of Chu] looks to Heaven; the worship of King Wen in the Hall of Light looks to the Lord on high." This is confirmed in the *Chong Yong* (19): "through the sacrifices of *kiao* and *shö* one pays homage to the Sovereign Lord."

The Hall of Light, *Ming t'ang*, is the ancestral temple. It derives from the bachelor house (*andreion* in Greece) of primitive societies, in which the warriors and hunters gathered. Expeditions still departed from it and returned to it in the time of Confucius. In all the liturgies it was therefore certainly God who was the object of adoration. Chinese thought is sufficiently explicit on the point. It is true that it preferred to use the term *T'ien* (Heaven) rather than *Ti* (Supreme Lord). But the *She king* often uses them interchangeably.

127

THE NATURE OF MAN AND
THE DECREE OF HEAVEN

■ "One can hear the Master speak of literature," Tse-Kong said. "One does not have the opportunity to hear him speak of the nature of man and the Way of Heaven" (*L.Y.*, V, 12).

At the very least, this means that these problems were among the preoccupations of his disciples. The *K'ong-tse Kia-yu* (*Remarks of the Family of Confucius*), which seems to expand on earlier succinct statements, tells us, "What one separates from the *Tao* [the Way] is the *ming* [the decree of Heaven]: in its unitary form, it is the *sing* [the nature of man]; in its transformations by *yin* and *yang*, which produce forms and aspects, it is life; transformed to the ends of its appointed span, it is death. That is why the *ming* is the beginning of the nature of man and death is its end. If there is a beginning, there has to be an end."

The confused syntax of the passage makes it obscure. I have not tried to lessen its ambiguity. Thus, one cannot tell whether it is the *Tao* (way) or the *ming* (decree) that has taken the unitary form of the *sing* (nature of essence). The context, however, is a guide. The *ming* (decree of Heaven, or occasionally of the Lord) is the *Tao* seen no longer in its mystery, its profound serene reality, but from the point of view of its influence. It is this decree that gives birth to the nature or essence of man, which has a unitary form or a form from the point of view of the unity of the beginning of which Confucius spoke. Moreover, "unitary" can have two interpretations: common to all men, or one with the *Tao* (as in the pairing of *atma-brahma*).

Confucius had to attain the age of fifty in order to understand what the decree of Heaven was. And he understood it through that non-conceptual knowledge that makes truth a certainty, that is science and wisdom, meditation and life, silent inaction and powerful action. He understood because he was at the center of himself, *chong*, in harmony with the purity and unity of his original nature. He understood the imperious moral exigency that came from his nature and, at the same time, the fact that there is an order in time that man must examine with reverence and to which he must conform and submit.

"That life be used is the decree; that the way be abandoned is [also] the decree" (*L.Y.*, XIV, 38).

WORLDLINESS AND UNWORLDLINESS

■ It is of course difficult to make a coherent, systematic presentation of a philosophy that has rejected system. It is still more difficult to characterize it in a word. There is nothing that one can say about it that would not be to some degree unjust. Nevertheless, there is a traditional Chinese differentation that seems exaggeratedly modern: the differentiation between worldly doctrines, *ju sheu* (literally, "entrance into the world"), and unworldly doctrines, *ch'u sheu* ("departure from the world"). It marks the division between Confucianism on the one side, and Taoism and Buddhism on the other.

Like all classifications, it is convenient and no more. In reality there is a common basis to Chinese thought. Taoism and Confucianism are equally concerned with politics. Each is based on a certain conception of the universe. Granet has shown that differentiation between the schools is anything but easy. Both tended toward syncretism, and each offered itself as a panacea. But it is true that the Taoists preferred to remain in retreat and did not believe in equity and the rites, and that Confucius coursed the world in order to attempt to reform it. In the course of his wanderings, it will be remembered, he encountered a certain number of "hidden sages." These would be classified in the category of the "unworldly." There were seven of them in his time. Some, Confucius tells us, had fled the world because of its corruption, others because of disorders, still others because of a word (*L.Y.*, XIV, 39, 40). The difference between them and him was one not so much of conception as of a different practical appraisal of the situation. It was the determination to restrict its field that made Confucianism appear so different from Taoism. In this connection the *Chuang-tse* has Confucius rightly say, "Those men [the Taoists] operate beyond the rule of life. As for me, I function within the limits of that rule."

It is on the plane of moral practice that Confucius must be judged. This was his strong point. On this plane Confucianism represents an enterprise in adjustment to the world. The Confucian can behave like a hero in it. His soul is not oriented

THE CONFUCIAN MODERATES HIS DESIRES
IN ORDER TO INCORPORATE HIMSELF INTO THE WORLD . . .

toward the beyond, the misty peaks into which the universe fades, toward that something or someone that is himself even while it is more than himself, through which, in a strange dialectic, his existence is corroborated, revalidated, centered, and unified. His morality seems to lack a central core and, as Hegel has observed, a certain internality.

He lacks a unifying force, such as that given by the prophetic religions. The plurality of the individual's souls in Chinese belief, which could be compared with a certain propensity toward superstition, demonstrates this fact. (Although superstition can be brought within the defense that Nietzsche adduced for polytheism: that it is the sign of psychic vitality.) If the Confucian moderates his desires, he does so precisely to the

THE BUDDHIST UPROOTS DESIRE
IN ORDER TO ESCAPE THE WORLD . . .

empirical degree at which they do not prevent him from incorporating himself into the world. He is not like the Buddhist, who kills desire in order to escape from the world, or the Puritan, who masters desire in order to subjugate the world to God. By not attaching himself to some transcendent object, he seals himself into the world.

THE PRACTICAL CHARACTER OF THE TEACHINGS OF CONFUCIUS

■ We are so accustomed to the concept that every morality is a theory of human conduct that it is necessary to emphasize the practical character of the teachings of Confucius. What mattered to the Master of Lu was the effective realization of virtue and morality in his own person and action. For him it was not enough to convince his spirit and his will: he strove to bring into it his whole being through patient, methodical labor. Truth was put into the service of this end. Therefore, the utterances of Confucian teachers are more like exhortations than theoretical explanations. They come forth in connection with a fact, a gesture. They seek to have a disciplinary, liberating force. They are inspired by the sentiment of a task burdened with difficulties, a serious obligation, a responsibility that allow no rest.

The Chinese language takes part in this task, if indeed it does not direct it. It has a great power of persuasion, musical in character. In fact, it embraces tones that in the last analysis are reduced in a sentence to a succession of strong and weak stresses. Each word has many meanings, and the imprecision of the syntax makes Chinese texts more literary than really philosophical. They preserve more of the multivalent power of emotion and the polyphony of concrete life. A translation from Chinese into a Western language, therefore, is like the translation of a poem by Apollinaire into prose. Comparison between the Sinitic and Indo-European languages, if it did not suggest that every body of thought comes down to its language, might at least add weight to the idea that many forms of thought, or what we take to be such, are merely forms of language, that properly speaking they are without content, that they are auto-productions of the language.

SECTS AND SCHOOLS

■ Chinese feudalism perished in the middle of the third century B.C. The Ts'in Dynasty founded the empire in 221 B.C., and the former Count of Ts'in assumed the title of She Huang-ti, "the first Emperor of Ts'in." This Dynasty was short-lived, ending in 206 B.C. The credit for stabilizing the new order of things belongs to the Han Dynasty.

In order to put an end to all opposition, and accomplish the psychological unity of China after having achieved its physical unification by fire and sword, the First Emperor, acting on the

135

counsel of Li Sseu, decreed in 213 B.C. that certain books be burned. The volumes in the imperial library and the technical works on divination, medicine, agriculture, etc., were excepted from the order, but the troubles that accompanied the transition from the First to the Second Dynasty seemed more disastrous, and the capital in which the Great Emperor had assembled unimaginable marvels was sacked and burned on a number of occasions. The first centuries of the Hans, under whom the proscription of the books was finally lifted in 191 B.C., were therefore devoted to scholarly endeavor, aimed at the reconstitution of the books that had been lost or destroyed. Such a state of affairs, of course, encouraged forgers: Lieu Hiang and Lieu Hin, who were major publishers of texts, were suspected of having falsified many of them. Furthermore, since the books of the time consisted of sheets of wood or bamboo bound by cord (some may also have been written on silk or silk paper), they tended to deteriorate, and hence confusion was unavoidable. This may be the reason for the apparent incoherence of many of them. Finally, having been put out of power by the first emperors, the Confucians soon regained it in large number, and Confucianism became a state doctrine. Under the guidance of the Confucians, the task of reconstructing the books was to be carried out in one direction only, to the detriment of the other schools. The "discourses of the hundred schools" had necessarily to suffer thereby, and it is difficult to arrive at an accurate idea of them.

In his *Han shu* (*History of the Hans*), the historian Pan Ku (A.D. 32–92) divided the thinkers of the feudal period into ten groups: the School of the Scholars (the Confucians), the School of Tao (the Taoists), the School of *Yin* and *Yang* (astrologers and geomanticists), the School of the Laws, the School of Names (logicians and sophists), the School of Mö-tse, the School of the Diplomats, the School of the Agriculturists, the School of the Story-Tellers, and an eclectic group of miscellaneous writers.

136

In this classification, as we can see, there was nothing methodical. In actuality the idea of a school as we understand it had little meaning in China: it presupposes a body of thought of a systematic nature that tends to assume the form of a closed universe. This is the case in Western thought, in German thought in particular, and is also true of Indian thought. In fact, it is a common characteristic of the Indo-European linguistic world and is peculiar to inflected languages. Just as the Chinese language lends itself poorly to rigorous conceptualization and is not favorable to logic, the Chinese mind tends to neither philosophical nor religious systems. It falls naturally into pragmatism and empiricism, and from the religious point of view it maintains contact with what we call the magic consciousness, which at bottom is a mysticism of action even before it is a humanist and universalist mysticism. The shapes of doctrines, therefore, are not clearly portrayed. Occasions arise in which opposing schools borrow arguments and ideas from one another with a view to syncretism; there are exchanges of "know-how," procedures, prescriptions. As is true of the Hindu *guru*, but in a very different spirit, in the last analysis it is the person of the teacher that stands surety for the teaching, that contains within itself the mysterious wisdom and irradiates it round him, in exactly the same fashion as the silent virtue of King Shuen.

The school was obviously framed on the feudal pattern. The candidate entered it as he became a client of his lord. After a fast of purification, the disciple was admitted to the master's table. The pupil became the teacher's *men-jen*, the man who stood at the gate. It was there that the master, facing southward like a prince, before the second inner court, carried on his teaching. A bond of vassaldom was established between teacher and disciple. This was the origin of the important rank that Confucianism gave to the master: immediately below the prince and above the father. But just as the masters traveled in order to engage in tournaments of talent with their competitors, so too the disciple journeyed through the world in search of masters from whom he could learn some secret prescription for knowledge and wisdom.

THE ORIGINS

■ It would appear that all the schools of thought derived initially from two official functions, the *shu*, 祝 and the *sheu*, 史 . The first was in charge of "heavenly affairs," the second of "human affairs." The jurisdiction of the former included services of worship, prayers, divination, and the calendar; that of the second extended to the recording of the king's deeds, among other things—historiography. In short, on one side there was the priest (or the sorcerer) and on the other there was the clerk or scribe. The priests were responsible for *Y king* and the clerks for all the other classics: *She king, Shu king, Li Ki.* In more remote times, under the Chang Dynasty, the *sheu* was the score-keeper in archery contests. These scribes were chosen from the lowest rank of the nobility, the *she* (not to be confused with the *sheu* 士 , which corresponded to the knights of Europe.) A special functionary, the *sseu-tu*, was responsible for recruiting them and placing them in scribes' schools.

All the schools of thought fell into one or the other of these two basic tendencies or were products of combinations of them. Thus, the School of Confucius was descended from that of the scribes (or annalists), the School of Mö-tse was descended from both, and Taoism imbibed the most varied currents. On the next page I have reproduced a diagram, inspired by that of Hsu Ti-shan, that was published in the *Yenching Journal* in

December, 1927, and used by Marcel Granet in *La pensée chinoise* (*Chinese Thought*) on page 7. It goes without saying that the diagram has a certain artificiality, and that it does not eliminate the need to discuss the doctrines.

Priests and soothsayers		Scribes and annalists
	Y king	
Numbers the calendar	Mö-tse	Confucius
Magic Medicine Elixir of life		Legists Logicians
	Taoism	

TAOISM

■ Confucianism and Taoism represent the two great currents that have coursed victoriously through all Chinese history. We have shown that they are born of a common source of naturism, but the Taoist flees the world in search of personal freedom and power that come from nature. He submerges himself into the mystery of nature. In this he differs from the Buddhist, for whom the universe has the character of illusion, *maya*. The Taoist represents the dark face of China, the underground current of dream and mystery. Occasionally he emerged into politics, as in the Yellow Turban movement of the second century. Taoism is full of preoccupations with medicine, dietetics, sexual hygiene, magic, and search for the pill of immortality (cinnabar). But it found its mystical and metaphysical expression in Lao-tse, in the *Tao Tö king* (*The Way and Virtue*), and in a great thinker and great writer, Chuang-tse.

CONFUCIUS   LAO-TSE

The personality of Lao-tse ("the Old Master") is not at all
well known, and this is not in opposition to the Taoist ideal of
an obscure and secret life. His name was supposedly Lao Tan
or Li Eul. Maspéro proposes the notion that he might have had
some connection with a Viscount of Tan, and Chinese scholars,
corroborated by Homer Dubs and supported by Duyvendak,
make him the father of the Viscount of Tuan-Kang, a general in
Wei about 273 B.C. Those who follow tradition regard him as
an older contemporary of Confucius. Relying on analysis of his
thinking, scholarly criticism places him at the junction of the
fourth and third centuries B.C. The *Tao Tö king*, the title of
which supposedly dates from the sixth century A.D., seems to
have been a breviary composed much later than his time—
approximately two centuries after the beginning of the Christian era, according to Herbert Giles: after the introduction of
Buddhism into China. At first glance it appears to be a com-
posite. The diversity of its styles, in both language and thought,
is immediately apparent. Some parts of it may have been
ancient hymns favored by certain mystic sects and deriving
from the old schools of divination. Many elements in it seem

140

to have been borrowed from the *Y king*. It contains that idea that has been thought of as uniquely Confucian: *chong*, the mean. Once again, then, we see a proof of the existence of a common store of Chinese thought. "Multiplicity of words will not exhaust the subject; nothing is so important as observing the mean" (*Tao Tö king*, V, in the text established by Duyvendak, Paris, 1953). It contains what seems to be, as Maspéro has called it, the avowal of a "melancholy mysticism."

> Others rejoice gladly, as if to celebrate a great sacrifice or ascent to a terrace in spring. I alone remain calm, like a suckling that has not yet learned to smile, abandoned like someone who does not know where to turn. Others have wealth in great abundance; I am like someone who has lost everything. I have the heart of an imbecile and a fool. Others are enlightened; I am in darkness. Others see clearly; I am myopic, weak and pale like the moon in its last quarter, wandering as if I did not know where to establish myself. All others excel in something; I am as ignorant as a peasant. I am different from other men in that I value the nutriment of the Mother [of the ten thousand beings].

The essential starting point for the understanding of all the rest seems to be an ancient hymn that demonstrates the profound character of the *tao* (the Way), its supraconceptual, intuitional nature.

"The Way that can be traced is not the eternal Way. The name that can be named is not the eternal Name. Unnamed, it is the beginning of heaven and earth. Named, it is the limit." Duyvendak, the Dutch Sinologist, recently proposed a different translation of this highly important passage: "The Way that is truly the Way is different from a constant Way." On the basis of a line from the *Hi-tse*, "A *yin*, a *yang*: that is the *tao*," he sees in it a philosophy of alternation. But this line itself is open to various interpretations. Does it mean a sum: *yin* +

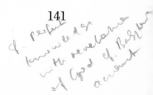

$yang = tao?$ or an alternation of periods: a time of yin, then a time of $yang?$ Or is the tao the medium within which yin and $yang$ move?

The truly great man of Taoism was Chuang-tse, or Chang Chu (second half of the fourth century B.C.), who was also called the Master of Nan-hoa, from the name of the mountain where he had established his residence. He was a story-teller of remarkable spirit. His work, which has been almost completely authenticated, is filled with the wind of the great cosmic spaces of poetry and metaphysics. He does not know whether he is a butterfly that dreams that it is Chuang-tse or Chuang-tse who dreams that he is a butterfly. Joseph Baruzi, the late French philosopher and poet, was inspired by this speculation to a very beautiful poem.

The *Lie-tse*, attributed to a legendary figure, Lie Yu-k'u, is a late compilation that would appear to date from the end of the third century B.C. It contains eight sections going back to the Han period, the seventh of which, from the middle of the fourth century B.C., is devoted to a curious personage, Yang-shu. A pessimist and a nihilist, he looked on everything as useless. The greatest sage, he said, cannot command even a single sheep. The legendary King Yu, who wore the hair off his legs in the service of his people, damming the waters of the flood, was just as mad as the tyrants Kie and Chu, who exhausted themselves in evil. All of them were thrown together in the nothingness of death.

Taoism is rich in poetic themes, and the philosophy is found in the writing of a poet like K'iu Yuen (c. 332–295 B.C.), or even in a Confucian thinker and statesman who was also a poet, Wang An-she (1021–1086 A.D.), who is regarded as the father of Chinese Socialism. The themes of the isles of paradise, of the terrace where the immortals drink, of the solitary fisherman lost in the fog and the waves are often the inspirations of Chinese painting.

142

漆園吏像

THE SCHOOL OF MÖ-TSE

■ Mö-tse, or Mö Ti, Master Mö, enjoyed a sudden resurgence of popularity in Chinese intellectual circles in the early part of the twentieth century. They found in him a way of thought that was closer to that of the West in its theism and humanitarianism. They would have liked to see him as an ancestor of Rousseau.

Mö-tse was almost a contemporary of Confucius, and their two schools have sometimes been classified in a single group, the *ju mö;* the Confucian disciple Meng-tse was to complain bitterly of the great number of partisans of Mö-tse not long afterward. He lived between 480 and 400 B.C., preaching universal love, *kien ngai,* and equality of property, *kien li,* assured by a despot who would enforce the law to the letter. He denounced war and military glory. All luxury was to be avoided and life was to be simple and frugal. This rather brusque utilitarianism of economic orientation was the inspiration of the totalitarianism of the Legists and gave rise to a strictly organized sect comparable to the terrible sect of the *Hashishin** in Persia. One anecdote gives a quite adequate picture of Mö-tse. He was asked why he exhausted himself running after men. "A pretty girl stays at home and takes care not to go out," he replied. "She is sought after. We live in a corrupt age. There are many who will go looking for a pretty girl . . . Few will take the trouble to look for righteous people. Therefore, one must do violence to people in order to obtain a hearing."

The work to which his name is given, the *Mö-tse,* is a quite accurate reflection of the tendency of his sermons. He preached to the popular classes, and shows that the concept of "the people" started to appear on the stage of history in the time of Confucius.

---

* The Assassins, who supposedly carried out their terrorist activities under the influence of hashish.—Tr.

■ In recent years there has been a great deal of discussion of the Legists, at least in Europe, probably because of the development of totalitarian systems. The doctrine is traced back to Kuan Chong, one of the ministers of Ts'i in the seventh century B.C., for whom Confucius had both praise and blame. He seems to have been no more concerned than his successor, Yen Ying, with the rites and the past. His concerns were economic above all. Unfortunately, the work that bears his name, *Kuan-tse*, appears to be a later forgery.

Shortly before the time of Confucius, for reasons that seem to have been chiefly fiscal, Tse-ch'an, Prime Minister of the state of Cheng, undertook daring agrarian and military reforms about 542 B.C., and seven years later he ordered that the laws be engraved on all copper pots. Both actions aroused sharp indignation among the feudal aristocracy. On the other hand, he had won the sympathy of the people. He was a man whose name was spoken with respect by Confucius. His reforms apparently were the result of pressure by external circumstances that compelled the little state to seek more food and troops.

But the great names of the Legist school, *fa kia*, appeared later. Kong-suen Yang, or Wei Yang, lived in the fourth century B.C. A minister in Ts'in, he was supposedly responsible for the elimination of the feudal system there (c. 359). But his end was tragic. Appointed lord of Shang in 340 B.C. after a military victory, he was later dismembered as a result of the vengeance of a crown prince who had become duke and whom he had forced to respect the law. The *Shang-tse*, which was translated by Duyvendak under the title *The Book of Lord Shang*, contains sections written at various times. It shows no respect for the customs of the ancients. Its author did not believe in the original goodness of human nature; a political realist in the modern sense of the word, and an imperialist, he stood for the absolutism of the prince against the nobles, for the law and the sword.

Yen Wen-tse is an even less well-known figure. He lived about the end of the fourth century B.C. Even his ideological position is confused: he could as easily be linked with the School of Names or with Mö-tse as easily as with the Legists. The Taoists themselves speak of him with indulgence. "Throw off the bonds of custom, despise adornment, do not be inattentive to individuals, do not stand stubbornly against the crowd . . ." these were the rules that Master Yen Wen followed. Through him it can be seen that there was a connection between the art of naming, qualifying, and that of legislating.

The best known of all the Legists, because he was the closest to us, was Han Fei-tse, or Master Fei of Han. He was born about 280 B.C. to the princely family of Han, one of the three states born of the division of Tsin. Supposedly he followed the teachings of Siun-tse, the most remarkable mind among the Confucian successors. Fei served first in Han and then went to the "far west," to Ts'in, like Kong-suen Yang and many other men of the time who were beginning to see Ts'in as the future master of the Chinese world. He won the admiration of the future First Emperor in spite of the fact that he appears to have been a stutterer. But he irritated his fellow-disciple, Li Sseu, another Legist, who was also the Prime Minister. Fei was compelled to commit suicide in 233 B.C. He, too, viewed the holy laws and not the holy kings as the important thing. He was an advocate of public disclosure and impartiality in the law. Unlike Confucius, he would not have countenanced a son's refusal to denounce his father for theft, or desertion from the armed forces in order to care for an ailing parent. He had a modern, rationalized conception of economy and technology.

The spirit of Legism showed that a new China was emerging through the feudal struggles. The battle that Confucius carried on against the princes was finally resolved in their favor. But in the small states a moral ideal of ritualism with archaic tendencies prevailed. For military reasons the large states imposed revolutionary measures that assumed the character of a fascist kind of Socialism. Legalism was better suited to the government of things than to the government of men. A totalitarian conception of the state, like the Prussian state as seen by Hegel, was taking shape.

THE SCHOOL OF NAMES
(*LOGICIANS AND SOPHISTS*)

■ The idea of accuracy in identifications went back to Confucius. When the great Emperor Ts'in She Huang-ti standardized writing, the size of vehicle wheels, and measures, he was to inscribe on the pillars: "I have brought order into the mass of beings and subjected the records and the realities to the test: each thing has the name that is proper to it." And many Legists, like Yen Wen, also belonged to this school, when they did not go back to Mö-tse. On the one side there were the logicians and on the other there were the sophists. Hu Shih, the late ambassador of the Formosan government to Washington, devoted a book to them, *The Development of Logical Method in Ancient China*, which was published in 1922.

Two of the best known sophists were Huei She and Kong-suen Long. Both were born in Wei, where the former served as a minister under King Huei (370–319 B.C.). The dates for the latter are unsettled.

This school was characterized by unending discussions on the great unity, *ta t'ong*, and the small difference, *siao yi*, which are extremely difficult to grasp. Certain paradoxes are astonishingly reminiscent of those of the Greek Sophists, such as that of the arrow "that flies and does not fly"—Paul Valéry gave it a destiny in a famous poem—a paradox intended to demonstrate the quality of infinite divisibility in space. The paradox of the stick that is cut down an infinite number of

147

times (at what point does it stop being a stick?) is amazingly like that of the pile of sand that is known to every student of philosophy. In my opinion, the possibility of Greek influences should not be rejected. This was the time when Alexander was shaking the world and restoring communications between East and West. But other paradoxes have a more pronounced indigenous character. For example:

The white horse is not a horse.

A mountain is as flat as a swamp.

When the sun reaches its zenith, it reaches its setting.

The south runs without limit and has limits.

I am going to Yue today; I arrived there yesterday.

The extreme of largeness that leaves nothing outside it is one; the extreme of smallness that leaves nothing within it is also one.

Chuang-tse said of Huei-tse that he "wrote enough to fill five carts, but his knowledge was specious and his words were without substance." As for Kong-suen Long, he was invincible in argument but he did not really convince. The dialectical ecstasy that possessed them did not communicate itself to the Chinese.

THE POLITICIANS

■ The politicians, who specialized in foreign policy, were not far from the logicians. They were the theoreticians of a system of alliances, *tsong-heng*. The north-south leagues, *tsong*, were directed against Ts'in; the east-west leagues, *heng*, were inspired by Ts'in. The *Chan kuo ts'ö* (*Discourse of the Fighting Kingdoms*) dramatically portrayed the politicians in action. Among them one finds clowns, musicians, historiographers, astrologers, traders, even ideologists of every kind. Su Ts'in and Chang Yi, tacticians of politics hardly encumbered by

scruple, had invented the art of charming and flattering. Shen
Pu-hai, who was a minister of Han in the fourth century B.C.,
seems to have been a follower of the old magic theory of expedi-
ency. Our own time could learn much from them; or they could
have learned much from us.

TWENTY-FIVE HUNDRED
YEARS OF CONFUCIANISM

THE FIRST GENERATIONS

■ The death of Confucius brings us out of the period of
Ch'uen Ts'yu (722–480 B.C.). We enter what Chinese historians consider the darkest period of their antiquity, that of the
Fighting Kingdoms (403–221 B.C.), which was intellectually the
most fruitful in Chinese history.

It was a time of intensive mixing of classes, populations, races.
Non-Chinese regions south of the Blue (Yangtse) River and
other areas that had not been much civilized by China came into
Chinese history. More and more the feudal states assumed the

151

shape of nation-states, analogous to those of Europe after the Renaissance, and again after the French Revolution. They threw themselves into merciless conflicts with one another. Little by little the armed nation replaced the feudal militias, which were of dubious reliability and mediocre effectiveness. The privy council supplanted the feudal council, the privy councilors coming from everywhere. This fact was certainly at the root of the ideological ferment. As a sign of the new age, all the princes assumed the title of king, hitherto reserved to the Son of Heaven. The function of the noble clans seemed to have ended. The class whose sound and fury filled the two and a half centuries before the empire was the same as that to which Confucius belonged: intellectuals, ideologists, specialists, technicians, mountebanks, charlatans, adventurers of every sort, ready to play the part of counselors to any prince and any state that were willing to engage them. Some princes had as many as three thousand of them. The paternalist prince of the little feudal court gave way to the tyrant of the great imperialist state. The empire was taking shape. Until then, the opposing leaders of the Chinese confederation had been Tsin in the north and Ch'u in the southeast. The struggle for hegemony was to be narrowed down to Ch'u and the "far western" state of Ts'in, to which in the end the empire was to fall. Both were peripheral states of barbarian origin.

At the conclusion of the prescribed three years of mourning, the disciples of Confucius took leave of one another. Some entered the service of the northeastern Chinese states: Lu, Ts'i, Wei. None seems to have made a career of any distinction. Others, remaining at first at the Master's tomb in the hamlet of K'ong-li, established schools. There were seven of these. The personalities of most of them are known through their fleeting appearances in *Luen Yu*. Tse-Chang was frank, honest, brave, generous, and scholarly, but, according to Tseng-tse, "he would be incapable of guiding others toward humanity." Tse-Hia was elegant and eloquent. He won authorization from Duke Wen (423–387 B.C.) of Wei for the foundation of a college of doctors ("scholars of vast knowledge") who would study the classics. His interests were primarily literary and ritualistic. His school produced the two commentators on the chronicle of *Ch'uen Ts'yu*, Kong-yang Kao and Ku-leang Ch'e. But it was Tseng-tse who sired the best-known spiritual posterity.

TSENG-TSE, THE HEIR
(FIFTH-FOURTH CENTURIES B.C.)

Confucius himself declared that Tseng-tse was not a man with any great endowment of perspicacity. He seemed rather niggling and narrow-minded. But he was extremely serious, and he had a profound appreciation of the moral responsibility of the *kiun-tse*.

"The disciple of wisdom cannot be without a great and resolute heart. The burden is heavy and the road is long. Humanity is the burden: is it not heavy? It must be borne until death: is that not long?" (*L.Y.*, VIII, 7).

When Tseng-tse knew that death was at hand, he sent for his friends in order to show them that his body was intact. This was an important truth that he had to convey to them, he said, with the sincerity "of the bird's plaint at the hour of its death." In his view, the body that one had received in the cradle of one's parents must be placed whole in the grave. His teaching, in fact, dealt with filial piety. In it he sought the motivation for human activity, a means of bringing men to the path of virtue.

Our bodies are the forms that remain to us of our parents. Must we not then use respectfully these bodies that they have left to us? To behave without dignity is to act without filial piety. Not to serve one's prince faithfully is to be derelict in filial piety. Not to be honest in one's relations

153

with one's friends is to be wanting in filial piety. To be a coward in battle is to lack filial piety.

André Malraux has observed that a Chinese feels himself offended only in his family. This is the proof of Tseng-tse's success. The compilation of the *Luen yu* is ascribed to him or his school. A part of it as it exists today is due also to the disciples of Yu-tse. Tseng-tse is supposed also to have composed the *Ta Hio* (*The Great Study*) and the *Hiao King* (*The Book of Filial Piety*). He taught at Lu at the end of the fifth century B.C.

TSE SSEU AND THE JUST MEAN
(END OF FIFTH CENTURY B.C.)

At the death of Tseng-tse, Tse Sseu took over the leadership of the school. His other name was K'ong Ki: he was the grandson of Confucius, who said to him: "My child, why do you not study *The Odes?* They elevate you; they teach you to see, to form bonds with other men, to serve your father and your prince, to know the birds, the animals, and the plants" (*L.Y.*, XVII, 9). He is believed to have been tinged with Taoism. In actuality his thinking seems quite close to that expressed in the commentaries on the *Y king*. He preached the virtue of the mean, *chong*—balance and harmony. He paid tribute to sincerity, which he exalted to the dignity of a metaphysical virtue, that of Heaven and Earth themselves. He was a lyricist, and certainly one of the great writers of the school. His work was centered on the idea, of magic origin, that virtue's influence is silent, being in harmony with heavenly influence. Quoting the *She king*, he said: "*The Odes* tell us, 'Virtue is [light] like down. Even down has weight. But the work of Heaven has neither sound nor scent.' "

His work comprised twenty-three chapters; what is left of it bears the title of *Chong Yong,* usually translated as *The In-variable Mean (Chong* = mean, center; *yong* = constant, easy), on the basis of Tse Sseu's own explanation and the gloss by the philosopher of the Sung Dynasty, Chu Hi (A.D. 1130–1200). In spite of this, I translate it as *The Just Mean,* but I give "just" both its interpretations, and this translation should only gain by making it clearer to the Western reader.

He was still living, perhaps a hundred years old, in the last years of the fifth century B.C., when Duke Mu of Lu acceded to the throne, and he was honored at court.

MENG-TSE AND THE GOODNESS OF MAN
(372–289 B.C.)

Mencius, as the reader will have guessed, is the Latinized form of Meng-tse. His real name was Möng K'o, and his appellation was Yu. He was born in Lu in 372 B.C. on the second day of the fourth month, and he died in 289 on the fifteenth day of the eleventh month. His father died when Meng-tse was three years old, and he was educated through the efforts of his mother, who was diligent in protecting him against all harm: living near a market, she had observed that he liked to imitate the talk of the fishwives; immediately she changed her residence. Meng-tse had a talent for eloquence. After journeys in several countries of central and eastern China—Ts'i, Sung, Leang—in which he preached his doctrine, with no success whatever, he withdrew with a few of his disciples, such as Yo-ch'eng K'o, Kong-suen Chu, and Wen Chang, in order to write down the discussions that he had had. This has given us well-written documents of a certain scope. Extremely alluring in its thought, his work has assumed considerable importance by virtue of the fact that in the twelfth century Chu Hi ranked it among the classics.

Like Rousseau, Meng-tse believed in the innate goodness of

MENCIUS

man, and he had a long debate on the subject with Kao-tse, who believed that human nature was neither good nor evil: it was like the wood of a tree, from which one could make a spoon or a cup, or like water, which one can divert at will to the north or the south. Meng-tse picked him up on this and pointed out that water had a characteristic, which was that of flowing downward. It would do otherwise only when its nature was violated.

He counseled vigilance in maintaining the spontaneity of the heart. If one knew one's own heart well, one knew the nature of man. Knowing this, one also knew Heaven. The great man, *ta jen*, "retains the red heart of the child." This is accomplished by practicing humanity and the rites. Desires must be restricted and life must be simple. In everyone there is a spontaneous capacity to do good, *leang neng*, and to know well, *leang che*. All knowledge and all wisdom consist in recovering what has been lost, in re-assembling what has been scattered.

He was the first to stand strongly in favor of the nobility of character against social nobility, to declare that "the people is noble and the prince is a small matter." He showed great independence toward the princes of his time. One day he went to visit one of them, who told him to come back the next day. "To-morrow I shall be ill," Meng-tse said, and the prince received him. Meng-tse thereupon explained that as a subject he owed obedience to the prince, but that the order of rights and duties was reversed when it was a question of his quality of counselor and master of wisdom. It is to him, rather than to Confucius, that the adjective "democratic" can be applied without inaccuracy. He emancipated Chinese thought from the magic spirit and the feudal spirit.

He was opposed, however, to the undifferentiated love preached by Mö-tse and the nihilist individualism of Yang-shu. To him there was an order in love, as there was in society. Those who labored with the mind had the right to be supported by those who worked with their hands, and even to govern them. This was his reply to the School of the Agriculturists, which demanded that everyone bear an equal part in working on the land. He was opposed also to the Legists' love of standardization, and he supported the rights of human diversity, of which the social order was the expression.

His work contains an interesting reflection of the economic interests of his time. In this connection he revived the system of land-distribution called *tsing* that characterized primitive times. This system consisted in the division of a given area into nine equal rectangular parcels, each of which was worked in common by a certain number of families; only the crop of the middle parcel belonged to the lord. But what had been a necessary distribution of collective labor in the primitive agricultural communities became with him a kind of utopian socialism. Since he was eloquent and exerted himself to convince, it is rather difficult to form an accurate idea of his contemporaries from him. He had simplified outrageously when he described Tang-tse and Mö-tse thus: "Tang starts with self-interest. He would not tear out one of his hairs to build the happiness of the world. Mö loves everyone without discrimina-

157

tion. He would work his forehead and his heel to the bone for the happiness of the world."

Actually, Meng-tse belongs to the best tradition of Confucian humanism. He rationalized it and liberated it from the obscurities and the miracles of the magic universism of the *Y king*. His thought was very close to that of the French thinkers of the eighteenth century. It is well known that China had some influence on that period of French life.

SIUN-TSE, THE DISCIPLINED MAN
(c. 315–230 B.C.)

Siun-tse was approximately fifty years younger than Mencius. He was born sometime between 315 and 310 B.C. and he died about 230, so that he lived about eighty years. His real name was Siun K'uang, but he was also called Siun King, Siun the Minister, and Sung King. He had lived through the decisive events that brought the feudal world to an end and laid the foundations for the empire, a crucial period of transition in China's history. Born in Ch'ao, he went to Ts'i about 265 or 260; in about 255 he went to Ch'u, where, it is believed, he accepted public office. His influence is supposed to have been determining in the beginnings of Confucianism, but after the twelfth century A.D. it was dethroned by that of Meng-tse. He was much and unjustly attacked by the Chinese reformers of the late nineteenth and early twentieth centuries, whose dream it was to return to pristine Confucianism in all its simplicity, undoubtedly with the intention of finding in it some reflection of Rousseau and Montesquieu. In fact, he represented perhaps the most robust spirit of the Confucian school. It is impossible to decide to which branch of the disciples of Confucius he should be linked: some have suggested that of Tse-Hia. But on the subject of that master and several others he expressed himself with great vehemence in his chapter entitled *Fei she erh tse* (*Against the Twelve Masters*).

The shoddy men of letters of the school of Tse-Chang follow the way of [King] Yu and imitate Shuen. Being me-
ticulous about one's dress, seeing to it that one's face is
composed, saying nothing all day long—that is the activity
of the shoddy men of letters of Tse-Hia. Fearful, not daring
to do anything, unashamed, fond of eating and drinking,
pretending that the *kiun-tse* should do no manual labor—
that is the shoddy men of letters of Tse-Yeu.

On the other hand, he ranked Tse-Kong very highly, on a
plane with Confucius. He said of both of them, "They did not
have enough land to drive a post, but princes and dukes could
not be compared with them in glory . . . They were holy men
who had not enjoyed favorable circumstances" (*Fei she erh
tse*).

The work attributed to him embraced thirty-two chapters,
but only four of these seem to have come actually from his
hand. Like that of Meng-tse, his work contained a large body
of polemic, through which we can form some idea of the intellectual vigor of the period.

Emphasizing the positive element in Confucius, he made a
distinction between man's influence and Heaven's. It is useless,
he taught, to concern oneself with Heaven's desires. He did not
believe that Heaven rewarded good and punished evil. Man
should not concern himself with Heaven's mysterious task: it
was enough for him to consider his own.

> Instead of honoring Heaven, it would be better to devote
> oneself to producing the riches required for one's needs.
> Instead of following Heaven and adoring it, it would be bet-
> ter to utilize its decree for our own ends. Instead of hoping
> and waiting for the auspicious time, it would be better to
> make the best of one's time.

He strongly attacked the beliefs and superstitions of his day
and the trust in the "signs" shown by weather. To him there

was nothing remarkable in eclipses, comets, and meteorites. Public prayers for rain made no change in the weather, but merely embellished men's actions: only the people viewed them as acts of the gods. He did not believe in chronomancy, in auspicious and inauspicious times. It is not up to us to do Heaven's work, as a Tse Sseu would have wished, or to try to become its equal. We have our own work to do. At least on this point, he seems to have departed from a part of Confucian tradition dealing with the relations between man and Heaven. He drew closer to the Legists, two of whom came from his school: Fei of Han and the future Prime Minister of the First Emperor, Li Sseu.

His positive mind was opposed to the religious devotion of Mö-tse, the learned discussions of the sophists on description ("The white horse is not a horse," etc.), and the theory of Meng-tse on the limitation of desire. Desire to Siun-tse was a natural fact. It could be neither restricted nor eliminated. Its strength or its weakness varied with individual characters. But it could be channeled, brought under the higher jurisdiction of the heart and the reason. Reason dwelled in the center of the heart. Here for the first time we encounter a positive psychology of knowledge. Which seems to be the fruit of perception by the senses. There is apparently a theory of memory as well. Reason, *li*, has the capacity to group the contributions of the senses, which the memory retains, and to separate among them what is essential. It is like the prince in the midst of his people. "He sees everything as a whole," Granet wrote, "in reason a product of man's activity . . . and a beginning of objectivity."

Error is the result of seeing less than the whole. "The danger for man lies in the fact that the part conceals [the whole of] the Great Principle." Through the inter-acting influence of all things, everything that we do and all our habits direct us or orient us. They block the synthesizing and jurisdictional activity of the heart, or, as we would say today, of consciousness. That

160

is why the wise man, knowing all the peril that lies in wait for the heart, suspends the *tao* above all things, above the thought of the past and the future, above what is far and what is near, even above his own will, as if it were a precise scale that preserved the unitary life of the whole, the order and hierarchy of things.

He did not believe in the immediate good knowledge, *leang che*, of Meng-tse. Rather, he believed that in every man there were potentialities that could be realized by education. The synthesizing action of the mind was the fruit of study and work. It was the product of human work, the millennial labor of human civilization that disciplines the disorder of nature. Therefore he gave the rites and music their just place, and it was an eminent one. Moreover, to him the verification of all knowledge was to be found in action.

In many respects Siun-tse may be associated with the Legists. But his humanism and above all his belief in the superior man definitely linked him with Confucianism.

THE RESTORATION OF THE BOOKS AND THE CONSTRUCTION OF ORTHODOXY

■ During the last two centuries that preceded the empire, the framework of the old feudal society was badly shaken. The effect was the release of a great intellectual energy. What was left of feudalism at the beginning of the empire? It is difficult to determine. We do know that for two hundred years two families of very ancient lineage still refused to allow their daughters to marry emperors.

Lieu Pang, who became the First Emperor of the Han Dy-

161

nasty, was not like the First Emperor of the Ts'in Dynasty, who came from a feudal house. Lieu Pang came from the people— some said that he was a mountebank, a man "dressed in sacking." His career began modestly at the lowest level, in one of the militia forces of the time. It would have been impossible for him to rise without the tremendous vacuum that was left by the fall of the First Emperor of Ts'in, whose authoritarian policy was not suited to the temperament of a peasant people. The Han emperor was successful because he was himself a peasant.

He knew nothing of the Confucians, who had recently been the victims of She Huang-ti's repressions. Their attraction to the past was not calculated to seduce him. All sorts of superstitions, worships, and myths had invaded the empire as a result of its aggrandizement. Empress Lu, an intelligent and cruel woman, was interested in the Taoists, or at least in the elixir of immortality. But the Confucians possessed a corps of educated men fully prepared for the organization of a minimum of bureaucracy required by the government of a large empire. They possessed as well a doctrine of government that matched the needs of a stabilized system.

"Sire," a cultivated Confucian told Kao-tsu, the First Han

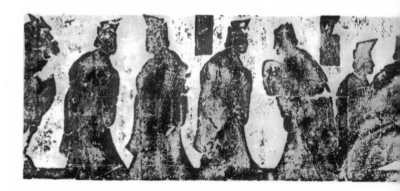

Emperor, "you can win an empire on horseback but you cannot keep it without a doctrine."

But it was only under the third emperor, Wu-ti (141–87 B.C.), that the disciples of the Master of Lu succeeded in establishing their authority. Furthermore, all the scholarly activity that followed the abolition of the ban on the books was complicated by the discovery of manuscripts in *ku-wen* (the ancient script). Intense discussions arose from the comparisons between these and the texts in *kin-wen* (modern script). The victory was gained by the moderns; or, rather, the arguments have not yet been settled. In 136 B.C. an Imperial edict established a college of Confucians, divided into five sections, each of which was assigned to the study of one classic. Eleven years later the empire established the system of examinations, what Renan called the "examinocracy," which was to spread orthodoxy as it grew; and both were equally dangerous to intellectual vitality.

In every domain the period was one of extreme vigor, which even now can be sensed by looking at the strength and movement of the Han horses in the frescoes, whinnying, snorting, and prancing; undoubtedly these horses came from distant Ferghana, and with them Wu-ti extended his empire to the west, even as far as the marches of the Roman Empire (which,

briefly, he thought of invading). The Silk Road brought China into contact with the West; of this there is a multiplicity of proofs. Chinese wood sculpture in the round is definitely related to that of Assyria. Alchemy was probably learned from Mesopotamia. The *T'ien Han-shu* (the book of the Dynasty of the earlier Hans) contains a strangely accurate portrayal of the Roman world, with the history of the Roman consuls who ruled in rotation. Jugglers entered China from the west in the time of Marcus Aurelius, probably from Syria. Another juggler came from Arabia. As in southern India and Indochina, Roman coins of the early Christian era (particularly of Pius Antoninus) have been found on the Cantonese coast. It is a matter of historical fact that in Rome Emperor Tiberius was constrained to adopt measures against silk and cotton in order to prevent a flight of gold. The wealth of the Chinese empire is demonstrated by the fact that in 123 B.C., after a victorious sally against the Huns, the emperor distributed 110,000 pounds of gold to his troops. And yet this was already the time when the empire was beginning to have recourse to monetary devaluation in order to meet the costs of distant expeditions. Proof of the peasantry's strength is the fact that it was treated gently in fiscal matters. Rather than create a tax on land, the government chose to levy on vehicles and boats, thus affecting the merchant class. In fact, it was fiscal problems that would bring down the Han empire.

Lacquer was widely known, and scholars have found the names of two artists on lacquered objects discovered in places as far removed from each other as Urga and Korea. Similar pieces have also been found in Afghanistan. Music seems to have experienced Greek influences as early as the feudal period. Dancing girls, as the terra-cotta figurines show, wore long, broad sleeves that they moved in time to the music. The harnessing of horses at the chest, the great importance of which in the transformation of medieval Europe is well known, was already depicted in bas-reliefs. The solar year was reckoned with precision to be $365^{385}/_{1539}$ solar days. The Chinese discovery of sunspots preceded Galileo's in 1613. A very sensitive seismograph was invented. Football was played by the armies. A lacquered chest shows us how women made up their faces: blue at the eyes, rouge on the cheeks, a beauty-spot near the lips. The great poet Sseu-ma Siang-ju (d. 117 B.C.) gives us some idea of the splendor of the palaces and imperial gardens, with their jade-encrusted columns, volutes and walls adorned with precious stone, and sculptured, painted, gilded wood. He himself amorously contemplated the empress from the lofty Orchid Terrace among the odors of strange trees, the cries of the peacocks, and the chatter of the monkeys. There is no reason not to suppose that Buddhism had already made its way into an empire open to so many influences. But perhaps a powerful empire was not yet ready to seek the consolations of Buddhist

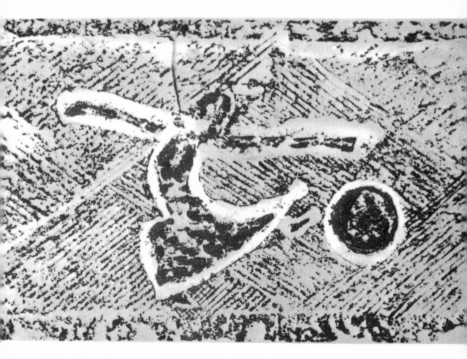

FOOTBALL (HAN PERIOD)

quietism. For that we must wait until the dark days that followed the fall of the Hans.

ORTHODOXY AND
THE THEORY OF OMENS

This was the time and the environment in which Tong Chong-shu was to undertake to establish the image of official Confucianism.

He was born in the vicinity of Peking in about 175 B.C. and died about seventy years later. Principally he studied the chronicle of *Ch'uen Ts'yu*, with a view to finding political precedents and a kind of jurisprudence in it. Naturally, he came to a scholastic interpretation of history, which made it possible for the corps of the cultivated Confucians, the possessors of this knowledge, to supplant the old nobility and to interpose themselves between the people and the prince as the interpreters of history, the people's will, and Heaven's at the same time. He was the instigator of an artificial, dangerous, and paralyzing theory of tradition that led as much to formalism as to a falsification of history. Thus, the vassal's sacred duty to reprimand became the educated man's right to censure the emperor.

In contrast to Confucius, who refused to discuss omens and miracles, Tong invented a theory of the signs of Heaven, derived from a certain interpretation of the *Y king* and from the little known doctrine of the school of *yin* and *yang* of Tseu Yen of the fourth century B.C. But in this instance it clearly assumed the character of a political method. A teacher of cram courses for examination candidates, he began his career with a brilliant literary effort for the competition inaugurated by Wu-ti in the first year of his reign in order to recruit "men of letters of vast knowledge." The emperor was pleased with this essay and subsequently suggested two further subjects to him. Tong immediately wrote two further essays. Their thinking was weak, but their rhetoric was brilliant with artifices. He wrote:

> I observe the relations among Heaven and Earth and men.
> This fills me with an immense dread. When the state is
> close to ruin because it has lost the Way, Heaven sends it
> reproofs in the form of calamities. If it does not reexamine
> itself (with a view to reforming itself), Heaven then causes
> strange and dire phenomena to appear in order to frighten
> it. If it does not improve, then its fall is imminent. So
> Heaven has great generosity toward princes. That is why
> it takes the trouble to warn them.

Tong proposed the establishment of an academy to train
men of letters, who would be resident students. Those who were
capable were to be directly appointed to high posts without
having to wait for the operation of seniority.

In spite of his politician's tendencies, Tong never held a
major office. He was connected with Confucianism through the
fact that he preached government by good works (*jen*) and
equity (*yi*), the rites, and music.

THE METAPHYSICAL AND SYNCRETIST MOVEMENT

Although they were of lesser importance in the orientation
of official Confucianism, the other thinkers of the Han Dynasty
were more interesting in many respects. Among them one can
recognize Taoist if not already Buddhist tendencies. Earlier I
quoted a significant poem by Kia Yi, whose *Sin shu* (*The New
Book*) is remarkable for the beauty of its style and the precise-
ness of its thinking. He had great influence in the court of Wen-ti
(180–157 B.C.) and was responsible for the adoption of yellow
as the Imperial color. He was born in 198 B.C. and died in 166;
thus, he came slightly before Tong.

Lieu Ngan (d. 122), who was related to the imperial family,

was the author of the *Huai-nan tse* (*The Master of Huai-nan*). He had assembled a certain number of philosophers round himself, and his work is the reflection of their discussions. It constitutes an encyclopedia of the knowledge of the time, comparable to the *Lu she ch'uen ts'ieu* of Lu Pu-wei (d. 235 B.C.) at the end of the feudal period. It bears the stamp of Taoist tendencies.

YANG HIONG, THE OBSCURE
(OR THE SOOTHSAYER)

Yang Hiong was born in 53 B.C. and died, it is supposed, between A.D. 14 and 20. He was a native of what is now Chengtu, in Sechuan. He held an important post during the interregnum of Wang Mang (A.D. 9–24), whom formal history regards as a usurper. Yang Hiong had nothing but contempt for the science of the commentators of his day. His thought found its inspiration in the *Y king* and also, perhaps, in the *Tao Tö king*. In other words, he was not in the pure line of Confucian orthodoxy. His book, the *T'ai Hiuan king* (*The Classic of the Great Mystery*), in which he set forth his metaphysical ideas, is obscure. It is a book of divination, and the fact that it was presumptuously presented as a classic brought derision from the cultivated at the time of its publication: the pretentiousness of Yang Hiong was contrasted with the modesty of his career. He replied with a pamphlet in which he said that men of genius ("holy minds") could be employed only in troubled times, and then there would not be enough of them, but that in normal times they were reduced to inactivity. There was nothing surprising in the fact that in spite of his knowledge he had not been able to find suitable employment. When Lieu Hin, a famous publisher (and perhaps something of a forger) of Confucian texts, had read the *T'ai Hiuan*, he said to its author, "You are wasting your time and your effort. Nowadays people

168

study in order to obtain material advantages. Already they do not understand the *Y king*. What do you expect them to do with the *T'ai Hiuan?* I am very much afraid that posterity will use it as wrapping for vessels of bean sauce."

Yang Hiong smiled but said nothing. Pan Ku, the historian, also rebuked him for his arrogance. Posterity was less ungrateful to him than Lieu Hin had expected. Sseu-ma Kuang (1019–1086), the great historian of the Sung Dynasty, took up his defense about a thousand years later. By then the book could not be found. It took Sseu-ma Kuang years to discover it. He read it some twenty times before he fully understood it. But in the end he declared, "Master Yang is a great scholar . . . Even Meng-tse and Siun-tse cannot be compared with him." Yang Hiong's other book, *Fa yen (The Word of the Law)*, attempted in its aphoristic format to imitate the *Luen yu* of Confucius. In other words, Yang Hiong's ambition was to be the equal of the great Sage of Lu.

WANG CH'ONG, THE STRONG MIND

With Wang Ch'ong (A.D. 27–97) we leave the mystical and metayphysical movement and return once more to the positive spirit of a Siun-tse. Wang's youth was one of poverty. Often he went to do his reading in the bookshops of the capital, Loyang. He was calm, serene, solitary, and contemplative. He held a very modest position, like that of a clerk, in one of the government departments. His *Luen heng (Discourse on Action)* comprised thirty books and eighty-five chapters. Another work, *Luen sing (Discourse on the Nature of Man)*, has unfortunately been lost.

He believed neither in God nor in gods. Taking up the old concept of *wu-wei* (not acting), which, as we have seen, was part of the language common to both Taoism and Confucianism, he endowed it with a new meaning. Heaven produces creatures without trying, through a process that is natural to it. That is why it is called "not acting." It has no thought. For, in order to have thought, it would have to possess the five senses. Heaven is so far removed from us that it cannot concern itself with what we say or think. Therefore it does not cause us to experience happiness or unhappiness because we have behaved well or badly. His line of argument was derived from a rather common materialism.

> The partisans of the theory of omens declare that man is in the universe as the fish lives in the water . . . But the fish influences the water only for a little distance round himself. Beyond that everything remains calm. Our influence is comparable to that of a fish. It cannot move Heaven.

Ghosts, phantoms, and assorted apparitions were the products of *yang;* since they lacked *yin,* they had aspects, *siang,* but no fixed shapes, and therefore appeared and disappeared instantaneously. Furthermore, they were the products of our illusions, the effects of disease or excessive preoccupation. Thus, when Pö-Yo made a study of horses, he saw nothing but horses everywhere.

On the other hand, Wang Ch'ong believed in fate. Our successes in the world had nothing to do with our talent or our virtue; they were predestined, inscribed in advance in our characters, and hence our appearances, the products of the unintentioned action of Heaven. Therefore a man's fate could be read in his face. For example, She Huang-ti had a prominent nose, long eyes, the shoulders of a sparrow-hawk, the voice of a wolf, etc. Therefore he was brutal and unattractive.

Wang Ch'ong professed no admiration for antiquity. In his view such admiration resulted simply from the fact that men despised what they saw and were impressed by things and persons of which they were told. Besides, writers like to embellish.

He believed in experience, results, proofs.

In proportion to its withdrawal from the old magic conceptions Chinese thought moved closer to positivism. It did not proceed in the systematic manner of the philosophers, but rather in that of the French moralists of the seventeenth century, who took as their basis reflection and day-to-day observation. Although it was a reply to official Confucianism, and in particular to the theory of celestial signs and portents, Wang Ch'ong's thought proceeded from the same spirit. The other scale in the balance was provided by Yang Hiong, whose thought was derived from the magic universism of the *Y king*. Clearly it was difficult for Chinese thought to emerge from these two fundamental themes. A true spiritualism was to be offered to it by India.

THE MIDDLE AGES
AND THE PERIOD OF ECLIPSE

■ The fall of the Roman Empire in the fifth century, as we know, initiated the era of barbarian invasions and the crumbling of power into feudalism, within which the medieval balance was little by little established in Europe. A similar phenomenon occurred in China after the fall of the Han empire. But in this instance, contrary to what happened in the West, the barbarian invasions followed the disintegration. The four centuries of relative stability under the Hans were followed for sixty years by the "period of the Three Kingdoms" (220–280). China was divided into three states: Wei in the north and northeast, with Loyang as its capital (220–265); Wu in the southeast and south, with first Wu-Ch'ang and then Nanking as capitals (222–280); and Shu in the west and southwest with Chengtu as capital (221–264). This period was made famous

171

by a novel of the same name at the end of the fourteenth century, which portrayed with remarkable clarity Ts'ao Ts'ao, a poet and the father of a poet, a wily politician and a great warrior. The unity of the empire was restored in precarious fashion for approximately another half-century, between 265 and 316, by the Tsin dynasty. Then came what is called the "period of the Six Dynasties" (316–590): six national dynasties south of the Yangtse River (in addition, there were four barbarian dynasties [at least] in the north, of Turkish, Mongol, or Manchu origin). For more than two centuries northern China was the Boulevard of the Barbarians. At the same time, as we know, nomads of the same stock, the Huns, were ravaging the Roman Empire from one end to the other.

However tragic the upheaval that arose from the collapse of a great empire was for individuals, it had some favorable effects on the renewal of thought and the progress of civilization. The whole architecture of orthodoxy that Tong Chong-shu had constructed as the foundation for the power of the class of the cultivated Confucians collapsed. Removed from power in an age of *condottieri*, they were ready to look for consolation in broader and more occult domains than those of official Confucianism, and to welcome new ideas.

Buddhism came at the right time. There are grounds for setting an earlier date than is generally ascribed for its introduction into China. It could be dated from some time in the fourth century B.C., after Alexander's conquest of the Indus basin and the creation of an Indo-Scythian empire in Central Asia. Given the missionary spirit that it evidenced later, it would have been amazing that between the sixth century B.C., when it came into being, and the beginning of the Christian era Buddhism would have made no attempt to reach China and that the Buddhist empire of Asoka (274–236 B.C.), which had won over Ceylon to Buddhism, would not have spread out as far as the Middle Kingdom. Moreover, the Chinese merchants who sailed the Indian Ocean between 128 B.C. and A.D. 6 could not have helped

173

bringing back from Ceylon something of the religion that dominated that large island. In any event, by A.D. 65 there was a
small community of Buddhist monks firmly established in the
northern part of Kiangsu, near the estuary of the Yangtse; it
was placed under the protection of the emperor's own brother.
The Imperial decree published on this occasion already provided an example of the transcription of Sanskrit terms into
Chinese characters.

But the translation of the Buddhist texts did not occur until
the arrival of the Parthian prince whom the Chinese call An-
she-kao, between A.D. 148 and 170. Born to the throne, he had
renounced it for the sake of his faith. On his arrival in Loyang,
he found a Buddhist community already there. Its activity
ranged from the capital to the coast. The translation of Sanskrit
into Chinese was accomplished in a curious manner through a
chain of persons: a Hindu recited and explained the *sutras,* a
Parthian translated them orally into Chinese to the best of his
ability, and Chinese who more or less understood him did their
best to reduce them to writing.

In order to translate concepts hitherto alien to the Chinese,
the first Buddhists employed a terminology borrowed from
Taoism. Thus, they were for a long time regarded as representatives of a Taoist sect. Inevitably there resulted a mutual infec-
tion of ideas and methods between these two doctrines.

Between the third and the ninth centuries there was no inter-
ruption in the progress of Buddhism. As early as the third century the landscape of China was dotted with those many-
storeyed reliquaries that are called stupas. Even today they are
still among its characteristic features. Missionaries came in
from Kashmir, Ceylon, Sogdiana,* Java, Vietnam, Cambodia,
etc.; chiefly, it would appear, from Iran. They brought with
them the two schools of Buddhism: *Mahayana* (The Great Vehicle) and *Hinayana* (The Lesser Vehicle). This opening of

---

* A region of Central Asia now embraced in the Uzbek Soviet Socialist
Republic.—Tr.

China to foreign influences was comparable to its opening to Western influences in our own time.

Its consequences were felt in all areas of life: medicine, mathematics—the discovery of trigonometry by Lieu Huei dates from 263—astronomy, music, linguistics, phonetics, and literature. Exactly as the modern Chinese have been compelled to create a new terminology for the translation of "electricity" (*tien k'i*) and "atom" (*yuen-tse*), the Chinese of that period, according to a Japanese scholar, Ogihara, created seven thousand new terms. Sometimes they rendered foreign words phonetically, in an approximate fashion. What is most interesting is the fact that, confronted with new ideas, they were induced to give some thought to their own and, confronted with a structurally different language, to pay greater attention to the problems of their own. Thus it was that before the fifth century the four tones were classified and a system of phonetic representation was invented by Shen Yue (441–513). This system appeared in two dictionaries, one published in 543 and the other completed in 609. What remains of them allows us to form some idea of Chinese pronunciation at that time.

Buddhism, as Goodrich ably summarized the history, introduced into China the ideas of *karma*, the transmigration of souls, the reward of good and the punishment of evil after death, an unbelievable quantity of heavens and hells, the measure of cosmological time (*kalpa*, 4.32 billion years), the world as illusion, life as an evil, sex as something reprehensible, the family as a hindrance to spiritual freedom, monastic celibacy, begging, charity, respect for life in all its forms, vegetarianism, asceticism, etc. Many of these ideas were profoundly alien to the spirit of the Chinese people, and it was never to understand them altogether. Even and especially today, Buddhist literature is a realm apart. Hu Shi was to regard the notions on the family and the illusory nature of reality, for example, as "bad ideas." In the last analysis it was the idea of escape from the world, release from the human condition, what Mircea Eliade

175

YUNKANG MUSICIAN
(WEI ART, SIXTH CENTURY A.D.)

calls the "deconditioning" of man, the reversal of the evolu-
tionary process into an involutionary process (which also op-
erates in yoga) that was to appear an illusion to the Chinese.

Buddhism succeeded, however, in introducing into Chinese a
spiritual dimension that it had never known before. It was to
emerge in painting, in those landscapes of mountains and
springs segmented by mists, in which the Chinese sentiment of
cosmic becoming was to be charged with unreality and infinite
compassion. It was to appear in the Wei statuary of the fifth
century, unearthed in the caves of northern China from Kansu
to Shantung, in the crypts of Tuen-huang, Longmen, Yunkang,

176

figures finely drawn with indescribable grace and fervor that René Grousset has compared with those of Chartres and Reims.

Buddhism was to find forms more appropriate to the Chinese spirit in the fourth century. Huei-yuan (334–416), a former Taoist, is supposed to have been the founder of what was called the Pure Earth sect, for which faith counts for more than works. The infinite evocation of Amitabha would suffice to gain re-birth in a mystic lotus in the Western paradise. The Lord of Light, Avalokiteshvara, of Iranian origin, was to undergo a strange transformation in this sect. In the beginning he changed sex and became Kuan-yin, or Kuan-she-yin, she who "hears the sound of the world," or rather its sorrow, before (some-time in the seventeenth century) putting on the uniform of a European warrior under Louis XIII. The worship of the *bodhisattva* Kuan-yin, holding a child in her arms, has often been likened to the cult of the Virgin Mary. She is the figure of mercy.

At almost the same time Chu Tao-cheng (397–434), a disciple of Kumarajiva (344–413), the great Indian translator, is supposed to have established the contemplative school of *dhyana,* which we know chiefly under its Japanese name of *zen* (*chen-na* in Chinese, *thien* in Vietnamese). Most historians, however, ascribe its inception to Bodhidharma, who came to China in 520. It is characterized by a method called "contemplation of the wall," and its goal is illumination. It was to influence the Master of the Elephant Mountain, Lu Kiu-yuen, in the twelfth century, and Wang Yang-ming in the fifteenth. According to this sect, Buddha is in every man's heart. Prayers, asceticism, and pilgrimages are worthless. In this connection I am reminded of two lines that I saw on a porcelain vase:

> *Let us laugh at those who scale the famous peaks,*
> *Unaware that Buddha is in their hearts.*

In opposition to these two schools there came into being the

so-called "school of T'ien T'ai," which was named for a mountain in Chekiang. It was founded by Che-Y, or Che-K'ai (538–
597), in 545. In contrast to the illuminationism of *zen*, it held
that study was necessary, and although it incorporated various
elements such as ecstasy, ritualism, and self-discipline, it de-
generated into scholasticism.

The troubles of the time benefited Buddhism and also Taoism.
One might say of the fifth and sixth centuries after the fall of
the Tsin Dynasty what Ngeu-yang Hiu (1007–1072), a historian, was to say of his own epoch: that its history could not
be recorded without beginning with the word "alas." Catas-
trophes of every nature compelled the small landowners to sell
their holdings to the rich at low prices. But then the new
owners, in order to avoid taxation, put the land under the protection of a Buddhist monastery or a Taoist phalanstery in
which they were careful to place some member of their families.
The poor grew poorer and poorer and more and more desperate,
and the rich grew richer and richer. In addition, the services
of all kinds that were exacted from the population, especially
military service, drove men to embrace the monastic profession.
According to Wei Shu (506–572), the number of monks and
nuns was estimated in his time at approximately two million
(out of a population that must not have been more than fifty
million in the whole of China, and he was speaking only of
the north) and that of the monasteries at thirty thousand. The
monasteries became extremely rich and drained off all the
country's precious metal. It was this as well as other causes that
was at the root of the anti-Buddhist reaction that surged up in
the middle of the ninth century.

The influence and success of Buddhism led Taoism to a
program of self-reform and the organization of a church. It
was in the eleventh century that the Chang family arrogated
the supreme Taoist pontificate to itself. Henri Maspéro met a
pope of this family in our own times, and the institution was
not officially abolished until 1927. Taoism was the faith of the

178

poet Tao Ts'ien (c. 375–427), whose works were translated into French by Jean Prévost, and the famous Lieu Ling, of the group of the Seven Sages of the Bamboo Forest, who made a reputation for himself with wine at the beginning of the fourth century, when tea was only about a hundred years old in China. The same tendency must also be ascribed to Ku K'ai-che (344–406), the painter of court scenes, one of which exists in the British Museum; his art points to a conclusion rather than a beginning.

The age was not favorable to Confucianism. From time to time, to meet the needs of the bureaucracy, a prince would remember to set up a college of Confucians or have the classics carved in stone; the number of men thus educated was not large. Even under the T'angs, in the eighth century, when Confucianism was resurgent, the number of candidates in state competitions varied between two and three thousand per session, and that of the successful between 5 percent at extraordinary sessions and 1 percent at regular sessions. Confucianism seemed irremediably bound up with the existence of a prosperous class that enjoyed leisure and prepared itself for the service of the state as others prepared themselves to work for their personal liberation. The Confucians of the period tended toward syncretism. Fu Hi (497–569), for instance, wore a Taoist bonnet, Confucian shoes, and a Buddhist scarf on his shoulder.

THE CONFUCIAN RENAISSANCE

■ After the centuries of historical depression, China returned to unity and grandeur at the end of the sixth century, first with the ephemeral Dynasty of the Sueis (590–618) and then with that of the T'angs (618–906). The Han empire was rebuilt. There was the feeling of a rebirth.

The overwhelming euphoria of the period found its expression in literature and the arts rather than in intellectual thought. We know the names of the two great poets, often mentioned together, Li Po (701–762) and Tu Fu (712–770). An anthology published in 1705 listed the names of twenty-two hundred poets. Wang Wei (699–759) was as great a poet as he was a painter. His poems were so many paintings and his paintings were so many poems—whence those poems that one sees in the corners of Chinese paintings. They were inspired by a deep feeling for nature (not the decorative nature of Rousseau), the joy and beauty of life, the melancholy of things that pass. The "pavilion of the golden crane," from which the sacred crane had flown, was evoked with mystic regret and nostalgia in the face of the "white clouds that float eternally" above the river of Han-yang. The blue fir tree in a moonlit landscape of sand and water poses the great enigma of creation. "What man was the first to look at the moon? What moon was the first to look at man?" The most popular of these poets was Po Kiu-Y, who, like Musset making Margot weep, made it his business to put nothing into final form until he had first read it to an illiterate neighbor woman. This was the time of the celebrated dancing girl Yang Kuei-fei, beloved of Emperor Ming-huang; she died tragically, "letting the golden bird that adorned her hair trail in the dust." It was the era when the emperor wanted to have a floor made of gold, with reproductions of lotuses, so that every step taken by the woman whom he loved would make a golden lotus bloom. It was toward the end of this period that that strange fashion of "small feet," which has persisted into our own time, sprang up among the dancing women. Ladies played polo, and we can see them doing so on certain pottery figurines. It was the era of the *vita mirabilis.*

The empire, practicing a policy of world-wide range, was hospitable to foreigners. The capital, Chang-Ngan, was thronged with Arabs, Persians, Tartars, Tibetans, Koreans,

FU SHENG, THE OLD SCHOLAR, STUDYING A COPY OF
THE *Shu king* (WANG WEI PAINTING, EIGHTH CENTURY A.D.)

Japanese, and Vietnamese. All kinds of cults were represented
in the empire. Zoroastrianism (or Mazdaism) is supposed to
have come in about 550, Nestorian Christianity in 635, Manicheism in 694 (this doctrine, it will be recalled, had briefly
tempted St. Augustine). Jews and Arabs were living in Canton.
Persian Jews had arrived even earlier, traveling over land. But
Judaism and Islam had no discernible influence before the
Sung and Yuen Dynasties in the twelfth and thirteenth centuries. Nestorianism has left us a pillar erected in 781, carved
in Chinese and Syriac, and a hymn to the Holy Trinity discovered in Tuen-huang. As for Manicheism, it had vanished
from its native country several centuries before it suddenly re-

182

appeared in China, to remain there for two hundred years before surging up again later, as if from beneath the earth, in the eastern Pyrenees in the form of the heresy of the Cathari, very certainly tinged along the way by Buddhism.

Sentimentally well-disposed toward Taoism by reason of the fact that the name of the Dynastic clan Li was the same as that of Lao-tse, the emperor was tolerant to all other religions, if he did not encourage them. Buddhism remained extremely powerful. Hiuan-tsang's remarkable journey to India in search of books, between 629 and 645, across the Gobi Desert and the passes of Hindu-Kush, earned further glory for China and renewed favor for Buddhism. The last major pilgrimage, undertaken by several hundred monks, was to occur in 966. After 1050 the triumph of Islam in central Asia cut off Chinese Buddhism from its Indian source. At the time of the edict of 845 against Buddhism, which ordered the return of a large proportion of the monks to secular life, the confiscation of the monasteries' wealth, and the destruction of the temples with the exception of those in the capitals and prefectures and those that were beautiful, there were still 4,600 temples, 40,000 altars, and 260,500 monks. In 1021, furthermore, this figure had somewhat increased: 397,615 monks and 61,240 nuns. In actuality, the edict of 845 affected all religions of foreign origin. The real reason for this anti-Buddhist reaction was the monasteries' wealth in metal.

On various occasions voices had been raised against Buddhism. But after the eighth century the Confucian bureaucracy, more solidly settled, showed marked evidence of impatience. The misbehavior of the monks and the occasionally aberrant character of Hindu "religiosity" provided them with a pretext, if not a reason. Han Yu (768–824), a writer of talent, who proclaimed his allegiance to Meng-tse, launched a very sharp attack on Buddhism. The emperor was staging a ceremonial to mark the reception of a relic of Buddha, and Han Yu declared in his petition to the throne:

> Buddha was a foreigner who knew nothing of the relation between prince and subject, between son and father. If he were still living, Your Majesty would receive him in the palace of Suen-ch'eng, honor him with a feast, give him a vestment as a present, and send him back to the West in order that he be prevented from perverting minds. How is it possible to preserve a dried bone of that man in the secret place of the palace? I petition Your Majesty to command that that bone be thrown into fire or water in order to destroy the source of the spirit of superstition.

This insolent memorial almost cost its author his head. It was very close to the point of view of Wang Ts'ong (584–616), who asserted two centuries earlier, "Buddha was a holy man, but his doctrine is not suited to the history or the climate of China."

NEO-CONFUCIANISM, OR THE PHILOSOPHY OF THE SUNG DYNASTY

In the beginning of the tenth century China fell back for approximately fifty years into a state of fragmentation, called the "period of the Five Dynasties" (907–959). Then the Sung

Dynasty was able to restore unity in a smaller China, until finally the barbarians, already established in the northeast, invaded the whole of the north. The Sung Dynasty, founded in 960, had to flee south for refuge in 1127.

"The T'ang dynasty," Thomas F. Carter wrote, "had been a period of expansion of frontiers and of contacts with the countries of the West, a period of freshness and youth, an era of lyric poetry and religious faith. The Sung Dynasty, cut off from the West by the invasion of the nomads, was a time of ripening and maturity. Lyric poetry gave way to scholarly prose—enormous compendia of history, works of natural science and political economy, of a character and a quality that had never been dreamed of either in China or in the West except for a brief period in Greece. Religious faith gave way to philosophical speculation and the great systems of thought that have dominated China into our own time. In art the lofty tradition of the preceding period was induced to bear its fruits, so that the greatest and best Chinese painting that exists today comes from the Sung period."

Buddhism continued to dominate the Chinese intellectual world. But after the persecution of 845, it would appear, only *zen* was left of the half-dozen sects that existed under the T'angs: T'ien T'ai, San lun, Avatamsaka, Abhidarkosa, Yogasara, Mantra; and undoubtedly *zen* survived because it was the best fitted to the Chinese spirit. An indication of the decline in the intellectual vitality of Buddhism: for one and a half centuries after 1037 there were no more than twenty translations (comprising 111 chapters) of the sacred texts, whereas between 982 and 1011 a translation service directed by three Hindus had published 201 texts embracing 1384 chapters. The First Emperor of the Sungs, moreover, wanted to reestablish classical studies in order to put an end to the reign of ill-educated soldiers. But most of the Confucian scholars had been schooled in Buddhism and had some acquaintance with Taoism, and neo-Confucianism was to show these influences. In order to find

SHAO YONG

CHANG TSAI

something equivalent with which to oppose Buddhism, they turned once again to that old book of divination the *Y king*.

Shao Yung (1011–1077) was a disciple of Ch'en T'uan, a Taoist or formerly Taoist teacher. He is supposed to have calculated the tropical year within four seconds. He had derived a science of numbers and a kind of physics from the *Y king*. From the unity of the *T'ai ki* came the two modalities of *yin* and *yang* to the infinite. The universe, *yu-chu* (*yu* = time, *chu* = space), was made of the same stuff as man. Celestial reason, *t'ien-li*, was in the nature (*sing*) of man. The two modalities were intelligent powers, persons in the sense in which we understand the word, possessing functions of guidance and judgment. They are reminiscent of the Hindu pairing, *Brahma-atma*. Sentiment (or sensibility), *ts'ing*, was what in man's pure nature reacted to the obscurity of things. It was like the moon, which reflects the pure light of the sun. It was the part of confusion. Therefore, man's true nature must be rediscovered and watched over even into solitude; then it would be possible to understand all things. Shao Yung's dialogue between a fisherman and a wood-gatherer is a famous fragment, in which he emphasizes the ineffable character of truth and the profound harmony of the universe.

186

CH'ENG HAO

CHU HI

To Chu Tun-Y (1017–1073), more often known as Chu Lien-K'i, "Chu of the Incorruptible Source," whose influence on his time was determining, *wu-ki* (absence of base, absence of peak, abyss) was the original foundation of the universe. In the language of *She king*, it had neither sound nor scent, no place, no beginning, no end. That was its state. In its manifestation it was the *T'ai ki*. These are the two faces of the same reality. The *T'ai ki* itself had an active and a passive aspect, or, as it would be phrased today, a positive and a negative aspect, constituting the two modalities of *yin* and *yang*, operating alternately to create the whole of beings and things. In the moral order sincerity corresponded to the second state, that of silence and tranquility, through which the mind reacted precisely to the truth of things, permitting proper and timely action. It is very well described in two lines from Chu Tun-Y:

> *Day after day I read the* Y king,
> *I do not know how far spring has come in my garden.*

Chang Tsai (1020–1076) went at the age of twenty to pay a visit to the learned minister Fan Chong-yen (d. 1052), who

187

counseled him to study the *Chong Yong*. Feeling unsatisfied with that work, he made a brief excursion into Buddhism and Taoism. What he called the *T'ai hiu* (The Great Void, or Indeterminate) seemed to differ little from the *wu-ki* of Chu Tun-Y. It lent itself to the same literary developments. To him, too, the *T'ai hiu* and the *T'ai ki* were the same thing, representing the negative and positive faces of the same fundamental unity of the universe. But what is the *T'ai hiu?* It is not easy to grasp a thought that does not define its terms (the remark is Granet's in connection with Chinese thought) or that takes pleasure in a hollow rhetoric (this observation is that of Suzuki) or that plays with verbal arrangements rather than with the arrangements of things, that indissolubly binds physics to morality. The *T'ai hiu* is not the nothingness of the Taoists; it is not the illusion of the Buddhists; it is simply something immaterial and invisible. The word that would translate it least badly would be "ether."

Like Chang Tsai, Ch'eng Hao (1032–1085) and Ch'eng Yi (1033–1107), who were brothers, belonged to the school of Chu Tun-Y. They were interested in similar problems. It would be tedious, even if it were possible to do so within the limitations of this book, to expatiate on them, but their concerns seem to have been about ethics. From the statement of the fundamental unity of the cosmos they derived a feeling of brotherhood extended to the whole of beings and things, and they justified the old moral conceptions that we have already encountered: humanity (*jen*), timeliness (*chong*) in action, sincerity, respect for oneself and others. To Ch'eng Hao good and evil were not absolutes; they arose as one did or did not attain to the just mean. And the problem was always that of maintaining a state of balance, of equanimity, which was the pre-condition of harmonious action, moral rectitude, and intelligence. Ch'eng Yi, who seems to have exerted more influence on the great man of the school, Chu Hi, gave knowledge priority over action. He recommended the radical examination of the

188

reason of everything, step by step, following a procedure that could be called analytical. Here one observes a reaction against the discussions of a Chang-Tsai, whose knowledge Ch'eng Hao called bookish, on the reason of the universe. It was by eliminating each factor, step by step, that one arrived at a unitary, synthesized knowledge.

The difference between the brothers is well summed up in a story. While traveling among the retinue of the governor of Han-Chu, one night they took shelter in a pagoda. Ch'eng Hao took the right-hand door, and everyone followed him. Ch'eng Yi entered by the left-hand door, and he was the only one to do so. "This," he sighed, "shows how I am inferior to my brother." His brother was friendly and tolerant, easy to know, while he himself was severe and solemn. "My brother can make others respect the doctrine of our masters," Ch'eng Hao said, "but, when it comes to guiding the young disciples, helping them to find themselves according to their capacities, there I will not admit to being second to him."

Chu Hi (1130–1200), a disciple of the Ch'eng brothers, was the most famous of the school; contemporary with the southern Sungs, his name was given to their philosophy. Proper in his appearance, calm in his manner, severe and respectful, he rose early and retired late. A great scholar, he was the author of many books, and he had much to do with the concept of Confucianism that is widespread today. He is regarded as the father of the doctrine of reason, or the norm.

> In the cosmos there are *li* [reason] and *k'i* [breath]. Reason is what is superior in the Way, the root of all living beings. The *k'i* is the inferior part, the substance of things. Beings and things establish their nature when they receive the gift of reason, and their visible form when they receive the *k'i*.

Opposite the school of Chu Hi stood his friend, Lu Kiu-yuen

189

(1139–1192), better known as Lu Siang-Shan, Lu of the Elephant Mountain, near which he lived. He established the unity of the heart and the universe. Without denying the part played by reason and matter in the formation of things, he gave primacy to the heart. It was through the heart that one loved and knew. Knowledge that went into details incurred the risk of obscuring natural "good knowledge," the innate "capacity to know," which everyone possessed. His thought seems to have been rather close to that of the *zen* school of Buddhism. It was he that Wang Yang-ming was to follow in the fifteenth century. He and Chu Hi exchanged an interesting correspondence. He was eloquent, and at a meeting that Chu Hi, then an official of the place, convened in a grotto to discuss the theme "the superior man loves justice, the common man loves profit," he moved his audience to tears.

All these men belong to the group of the conservatives, one of whose leaders was the historian Sseu-ma Kuang (1019–1086). One of their noteworthy opponents was the reformer Wang Ngan-she (1021–1086), or An-she, one of the most amazing men of the Sung dynasty: a great poet, a scholar, a statesman. His attempt at state socialism failed, and with equal unsuccess he challenged the exclusively literary character of the competitive tests—he wanted to replace these with questions on political economy, law, etc.

Neo-Confucianism, developed under the Sung Dynasty, has survived almost into our own time. Without it China might have become Buddhist, Moslem, or Christian. But it is striking to observe that in its battle against Buddhist metaphysics it could not do otherwise than turn back to the old problems of a universist physics born of a book of divination and magic. The spirit of magic and alchemy—as we see in Bacon—is closer to science than one would think, but in order to culminate in it experiment must be conducted in a rigorous conceptual system. This is the nub of the question. In spite of many important discoveries that she made ahead of Europe, China did not succeed

190

in constituting a body of science first, for the very reason for which she did not create a religion or a logic. In this respect her growth was profoundly different from that of India, to which we owe religions and the "zero"—the zero that Gandhi made the goal of his spiritual experience. Because the Chinese operate poorly in the abstract—and for this the language is to be blamed—they restrict themselves to the concrete and do not,

like the Hindus or Descartes, cast doubt on the reality of the world: hence they find the idea of deliverance from the world absurd.

COSMOPOLITANISM

At the end of the thirteenth century, China formed part of a vast world empire that ran from Vienna to Seoul. Under the *pax mongolica* the Silk Highway became Marco Polo's for twenty years. China was once more opened to all foreign influences, as under the T'angs. Guillaume of Rubruk, the emissary of St. Louis, is supposed to have been told by the Mongol sovereign Mongka, "God gives us many fingers on our hands. Thus he gives us many religions." China of that day contained Nestorian churches side by side with Catholic churches, mosques, synagogues, and pagodas. A Russian won the first prize in the state competition of 1231. Chinese engineers created the irrigation system for Mesopotamia. Chinese printing is supposed to have penetrated into Europe at this time.

It would appear that Confucianism does not find its best climate in periods of powerful new impulses. It was not persecuted; in fact, it enjoyed marks of favor from the government. But in the whole complex the Confucian bureaucracy played a subordinate part. It had a conservative cast, bitterly opposed to change; it was interested in morality and social stability in an age in which power politics was concerned above all with finding new science, art, and technique. It was in this period, however, that Wang Ying-lin (1223–1296) composed the *San tse king* (*The Three Characters*), a well-known textbook for children arranged on a pattern based on three characters, which was still being used recently in the schools of China and Vietnam. It began with a sentence that might have been a quotation from Rousseau: "Men are born good; contact with society makes them bad."

The traditional examinations having been held in abeyance over a period of seventy-eight years, from 1237 to 1315, the men of letters found the theater a refuge for their moral ideal (and perhaps too for their subversive ideas), and the Mongol period was the great age of the Chinese theater.

The Mongol Dynasty fell in the second half of the fourteenth century—in 1394, to be precise—after having reigned in China for more than a century, since 1260. It was succeeded by the Ming Dynasty (1368–1644). Although the founder of this house was a former Buddhist monk, he gave a place of honor to the Sung philosophers and especially to Chu Hi, probably because the Confucians had not held the foremost rank under the previous Dynasty.

THE SCHOOL OF THE HEART

But interminable discussions of the universal reason and the nature of man by men of science who, moreover, were principally concerned with passing examinations were bound to incite reaction.

The opposition was represented by Wang Chu-jen, more frequently known under the name of Wang Yang-ming (1472–1528). He belonged to the subjectivist movement of Lu Siang-shan and claimed allegiance to Meng-tse. Although he denied the charge, he was believed to be rather close to *zen* illuminationism. He preached the doctrine of innate intuitive knowledge, the "good knowledge," *leang che,* that comes from a naturally good heart, *leang sin.* There was unity between knowledge and action. "He who does not do does not know." "There are consonance and resonance of all beings among one another." (These statements are by Wieger.) Therefore, one must exert one's will in order to rid one's heart of what troubles it, to create silence within oneself in order to listen to it, "to keep pure and brilliant the mirror" of one's soul. There was no need to question books or other persons.

> *Everyone has a Chong-ni [Confucius] in his heart,*
> *Sometimes visible, sometimes concealed.*
> *Let us say directly what this means:*
> *Inborn knowledge and nothing else whatever.*

In consequence of the impact of the West at the beginning of the twentieth century, the school of Chu Hi lost favor among the cultivated Chinese; the whole current that ran from Mencius to Wang Yang-ming had gained standing with them. Another explanation for this school's success arose from the fact that its doctrine was dominant in Japan (in Japanese Wang Yang-ming became Oyomei) at the period of the decisive transformation of the Meiji era, but this was ascribing much too much to the influence of a doctrine in the evolution of a people.

In actuality the Ming Dynasty did not make any particular mark in the realm of thought, but rather in those of the theater and the novel. Thanks to the widely prevalent use of printing since the tenth century, saga novels like the *San kuo* (*The Three Kingdoms*), attributed to Lo Pen or Lo Kuan-chong (late fourteenth century), reached a broad public. This historical novel gained popularity for such figures as Liu Pi, representing legitimacy; Chu-ko Leang, the type of the invincible strategist; Kuan Yo, the incarnation of honesty (often portrayed with a red face, and worshiped in all the temples of Vietnam); and Ts'ao Ts'ao, the suspicious, guileful usurper, of all the characters the least in keeping with the Confucian ideal. In addition to the historical fiction, there were other novels that dealt, for example, with brotherhoods of "redressers of wrongs" like the *Shuei hu* (*The Strand*), attributed to She Nai-ngan (end of the fourteenth century), translated into English by Pearl Buck in 1933; with symbolic voyages of quests, reminiscent of the tales of the Holy Grail, like the *Si Yu Ki* (*Journey to the West*),

194

attributed to Wu Ch'en-ngen (c. 1500–1582), translated into English by Arthur Waley in 1943 and into French by Louis Avenol more recently, which popularized the Indian pilgrimage of the monk Hiuan-tsang under the T'angs; or with gods and demons. And, finally, there were some very daring novels of society and manners.

Far from the least amazing among all the literature of this period is a Chinese version of *La divina commedia* (cf. J. L. L. Duyvendak, *A Chinese "Divina commedia,"* in *T'ung Pao*, XLI). Much condensed, radically altered, naturalized Chinese, it remains completely recognizable. The reader meets once more Dante's *antica strega*, the tower to which the dead ascend in order to take a last look at the scenes in which they spent their lives. Its source was probably some now vanished travel tale by a Chinese voyager, probably a Moslem who had gone to Mecca. The Chinese *Divina commedia* was probably a contemporary of the great voyages into the southern seas and the Indian Ocean as far as the coasts of Arabia and Africa that were organized at the beginning of the fifteenth century by Cheng Ho, the Great Eunuch, and that gave rise to a large number of fantastic stories of ocean travel.

All these novels are worthy of greater interest than has been usually shown in them and than they received from the cultivated Confucians in particular. In spite of the excessive use of suspense and the frequently invoked appearance of the *deus ex machina*, they are rich in psychology and they provide a remarkable insight into Chinese psychology and the unconscious mythology that rules the Chinese. Kin Sheng-t'an (c. 1610–1661), who wrote prefaces for the *Shuei hu* and the *San kuo*, found more meaning and literary worth in them, in fact, than in the works of philosophy, poetry, and history. Admirable stories, compact and short, are infused with symbolic meanings.

Finally, carrying on a tradition inaugurated by the Sungs, or at least magnificently represented by them, the Mings distinguished themselves with encyclopedias, one of which, completed in 1407, was so enormous that it was impossible to publish it. It consisted of 11,095 volumes, containing 22,877 chapters; 368 of the volumes have survived. Among the scholarly works of various kinds we ought to point out a dictionary of 1615 compiled by Mei Ying-tso. It contained 33,179 characters and set the number of radicals at 214; previously the figure had oscillated between 540 and 544. In fact, it was a renewal of an attempt at scriptural simplification (setting the number of radicals at 242) undertaken by a Khitan Buddhist priest in 997. This is a problem that continues to clamor for the attention of the leaders of the new China. The number of 214 can certainly be reduced still further today. The woodcuts of the period, made for the illustration of the books, are extremely interesting.

WEST AND EAST

No one questions the fact that the major event under the Mings was the arrival of European missionaries. The most remarkable of these, or at least the first in order of seniority, was an Italian, Matteo Ricci (transcribed in Chinese as Li Ma Ts'eu), who was born in 1552 and died in 1610. Like Alexander of Rhodes in Vietnam, he adapted himself completely and quickly to Chinese life. He was regarded by the cultivated Chinese as one of them, and he found followers among them. He was followed by such eminent men as Adam Schall, Nicolo Longobardi, Jacques Rho, Sabbatins des Ursis, etc., as well as others whom it would be difficult to identify under the Chinese transcriptions of their names.

They adapted well to Chinese life because it was not yet far removed from Western life. It was to become so in the nineteenth century, after the scientific and industrial revolution in Europe. In the thirteenth century everything in the Far East was a marvel to Marco Polo. At that time no comparison was possible between a Europe emerging with difficulty from the night of the Middle Ages and the rich empires of Asia. But, between the sixteenth and seventeenth centuries, the scientific advances made in Europe and imparted to China through the Jesuits' translations of works of mathematics, astronomy, etc., began to surprise the Chinese mind. It was an imperceptible intellectual revolution, the consequences of which were to become evident in the nineteenth century.

Through the Jesuits, then, the Chinese glimpsed something of Europe's Renaissance. But China could not draw all the consequences from it. On the contrary, her power, incomparably greater than that of any of the European nations, prevented her from recognizing the new direction of the human mind. On the other hand, still through the intermediary of the Jesuits, China contributed to the acceleration of European progress. What she had of positivism and rationalism—somewhat limited, it was true, and enclosed in a context of thought of magic origin—determined the philosophy of the luminaries of the eighteenth century. There was an echo of this in Fénelon, who wrote a dialogue in which Socrates and Confucius debated; in Leibnitz, Beyle, and Voltaire. Voltaire—that meant something! Through a reverse impact, this French thought of the eighteenth century was to determine the whole Chinese reform movement that ran from Leang K'i-chao to Sun Yat Sen.

Between the last of the Mings and the beginning of the Manchu Dynasty (1644–1912) it is possible to discern Western influence in a series of Chinese thinkers. It aroused a reaction against the intuitionism of Wang Yang-ming and the metaphysics of a Chu Hi. Ku Yen-wu, better known under the name of Ku T'ing-lin (1613–1682), called for science founded on profound and extensive study, on analysis and proof. He revolted against a bookish science oriented solely to the imitation of the ancients. Repeating the ancients, in his view, was not worth the effort. He deleted from his *Jö che lu* (*Collection of Everyday Knowledge*) everything that seemed to him to have been said before. Yen Jo-kiu (1616–1704) was his adversary

in the same domain. Tai Chen (1723–1777) devoted himself to a harsh criticism of the texts. Mao K'i-ling (1623–1713) justified desire and life against metaphysical and inaccessible reason. Huang Tsung-hi (1610–1695) attacked the monarchy. Wang Fu-che (1619–1692) posed questions to himself on the methods and origins of knowledge. Li Kung (1659–1733) emphasized experience and specialization.

The mere mention of these names shows that Chinese thought continued to be active and progressive under the Mings and the Manchus. Nevertheless, it seemed to have had difficulty in liberating itself from a moral and political orientation.

A historian who looks for signs, if not for causes, in the complex history of man, which perhaps is to be understood only by millennia, believes indeed that he can descry vague symptoms of the future crisis of the nineteenth century. And yet, China was to reach her apogee with K'ang Hi (1662–1722). At the beginning of the fifteenth century Chinese navigation, going from Sumatra to Arabia, still dominated the Indian Ocean. The largest Chinese ships reached a length of 350 feet and had cabins with bathrooms; a fleet included more than sixty of them. But at the end of the century, through some strange dread, Chinese navigation suddenly was halted, and Chinese were even forbidden to leave the country. In a reflex that was evidence of some hidden weakness, the empire withdrew into itself. The reason must be looked for in the fear of the various pirates, some of whom were other Chinese. Their raids on the Chinese coast increased. At first the Japanese were the most active. Then, in the seventeenth century, came the Portuguese and the Dutch. A Japanese fleet in 1552 had the hardihood to sail up the Yangtse, destroying all the towns on both banks. The cost of maritime expeditions became intolerable for a budget that was constantly rising under the pressure of military necessities. The growth of latifundia, which had caused the downfall of a number of dynasties, did as much for the Mings. And, in accord with a familiar rhythm, it was once more a barbarian dynasty, the Manchu Dynasty of the Ts'ings, that replaced the indigenous Dynasty of the Mings in the middle of the seventeenth century, before itself being completely absorbed by the country, to which it brought definitive possession of Manchuria as a dowry. China has always grown larger by being conquered, and in her the conquerors lose even their ethnic identities.

Too chronological a history, however, would leave us in ignorance of facts of great importance, and not only on the material plane: for example, the sudden rise in the population in the second half of the seventeenth century. Between the seventh century and 1578, the total had ranged between 50 and 60 million. Suddenly it doubled, reaching 108 million in 1661 and 143.4 million in 1741. (In 1700 the population of western Europe, including the British Isles, France, Germany, Italy, and Austria, was 54 million.) This phenomenon was the consequence of the importation of maize and various other crops

200

and of the growth of commerce. The curious Chinese porcelains painted with scenes of Europe, manufactured with a view to export, like the later Japanese products of Yokohama, were proof of the importance of trade with Europe. Incidentally, it brought about a deterioration in the quality of this porcelain.

THE WESTERN IMPACT

European pressure began to become extremely strong after 1840, as a consequence of the scientific and industrial revolution. China did not know how to reply to it. "Incapable of seeing beyond the ends of their noses," Carrington Goodrich amusingly observed, "the court and its counselors attempted to practice a policy of isolation." Europe responded to this policy with insistence on the formula of the "open door and equal opportunity," which, in its second term, was an American policy.

The bewilderment of the Chinese spirit was manifested in

the work of K'ang Yeu-wei (1858–1927) and Leang K'i-chao (1873–1929). With an obvious awareness of the untimeliness of the challenge by which China was confronted and a lack of understanding of its nature, as the brilliant historian Arnold Toynbee has pointed out, K'ang Yeu-wei began with textual criticism, challenged the authenticity of the Confucian texts in *ku-wen* (the ancient script), and called for a return to the manuscripts in *kin-wen* (the script that was modern at the time of the Han Dynasty!), which were apparently simpler; thus he continued a tradition of exegesis that had been begun in the seventeenth century. In the *Ta t'ong shu* (*The Great Harmony*) he described a utopia that was half-Confucian, half-communist. Leang K'i-chao was a reasonably muddled thinker, although a brilliant writer. A disciple of K'ang Yeu-wei, he adhered briefly to the so-called "School of the Heart of the Master of the Elephant Mountain and Wang Yang-ming." Probably, under the influence of European thinkers like Huxley, Montesquieu, or Rousseau, who were being made known to China at about this time, he wanted to confront the West with a less esoteric China, stripped of the vestiges of Buddhism and the universist speculations of the Sungs, more democratic and tending toward socialism. To him Confucianism had fallen into a decline immediately after Mencius. Siun-tse in particular, certainly the keenest mind in the Confucian tradition, was the object of his enmity. He traveled to Japan and the United States, took part in a conspiracy, founded a newspaper in Shanghai, and engaged in ideological activity. His thinking led to the reformism of Sun Yat Sen, a rather weak but revolutionary thinker who has acquired the stature of a symbol to democratic China. One of Leang's books was translated into English under the title *History of Chinese Political Thought*.

After him, Hu Shi, who died in the beginning of 1962, was the author of a history of Chinese philosophy (1919) and an excellent book on the Chinese logicians (1922). He and Lu Siun, the future Gorky of China, established a literary school, from which Lu Siun separated in order to form another group with Mao Tuen. Kuo Mo-jo was one of the founders of a society for the study of Marxism. Fong Yeu-Lan is a broadly informed, though occasionally confused, historian of philosophy. Although he was not a Marxist, he rallied behind the new government of mainland China. But here we are no longer in Confucianism, at least directly.

Will Marxism be understood by the Chinese? Will it resolve the problems of Chinese thought? This book does not propose to offer any reply to that. But the experience of Buddhism in China offers some ground to suppose what the answer could be. What is abstract and systematic in Marxism, it seems, must remain alien to the Chinese mind. It cannot even be imagined that it will evolve a specifically Chinese Marxism as it created *zen* Buddhism, because Marxism does not deal with a reality that can be attained through nonconceptual channels. Dialectic or not, it is a direct descendant of Western rationalism; more or less implicitly, it carries forward the mechanism of things in the logic of the mind. Chinese thought, which occasionally evidences a positive, practical, pre-scientific, but concrete aspect, has its roots in primitive magic-religious conceptions, more magic than religious; whence comes its ritualism. Between the two bodies of thought there are encounters, but the gaits of the minds are different, and the incompatibilities are many. China could use Marxism, and indeed contribute to it the corrective of her own empiricism and humanism; the spirit of the system would remain alien to her. At the conclusion of his excellent little book on *la Littérature chinoise* (*Chinese Literature*), Kaltenmark-Ghequier has stated the problem with great perception: "The great drama of the new China is this: to become a modern nation without renouncing her civilization of many thousands of years."

203

CHRONOLOGICAL TABLE OF
CHINESE AND WORLD HISTORY

THE THREE VENERABLES AND
THE FIVE SOVEREIGNS
(legendary period)

Fu-hi (traditional dates:
    4480–4365[?] B.C.)
    Divination, writing, marriage, etc.

Shen-nong (3330–3080[?] B.C.)
    Agriculture.

Huang-ti (2697–2597[?] B.C.)
    Patron of smelters and the Taoists;
    calendar, medicine, family names,
    garments, etc.

Yao (2357–2257[?] B.C.)
Shuen (2256–2208[?] B.C.)

    Patrons of the Confucians.

THE THREE DYNASTIES

Hia (c. 2000–1523 B.C.)
    Founded by Yu the Great, drainer of
    the waters of the Deluge; end of
    Stone Age.

Chang or Yin (c. 1523–1027)
    Oracular inscriptions, animistic and
    orgiastic religions, bronze and marble
    figurines, etc.

Chu (1027–249)
    1. The first kings (1027–771): *The
       Odes.*
    2. Period of *Spring and Autumn*
       (722–481): Confucius (551–479).
    3. Period of the Fighting Kingdoms
       (403–249): Mencius (372–289).

Obeid period in Mesopota-
mia, fifth-fourth millen-
nium B.C. Sumeria, 3500
B.C. Cuneiform writing,
3000–2700 B.C. City-states,
2700–2300 B.C. Ur III, Neo-
Sumeria, 2000. Destruction
of Troy, 2200. Nile and
Indus civilizations at about
the same period. (Civilizations of Baluchistan, 3500–
3000; Mohenjo-Daro, 2500–
2000; Ancient Empire in
Egypt, 2800.)

Appearance of the Indo-
Europeans. First Cretan
palaces, c. 2000. Babylon
(1900–1800). Abraham.
The *Vedas,* 1500–1000.
Egyptian conquests, 1500–
1400. Birth of Moses, 1305.
Trojan War, c. 1200.
Phoenicians, c. 1000. Foundation of Rome, 753.
Homer, c. 740. Thales, c.
585. Pythagoras, born be-
tween 590 and 570. Hera-
clitus, c. 504. Buddha, 556–
476. Completion of Old
Testament, c. fifth century.
Socrates, 470–399. (Confucius contemporary with
pre-Socratics and Buddha.)
Alexander in India, 327–
325.

205

THE FIRST EMPIRE

Ts'in Dynasty (249–207)
> Distinguished by the great personage of Ts'in She Huang-ti (First Emperor). Legist policy. Burning of the books, 213. The Great Wall.

Consecration of Asoka in India, 260. Hamilcar in Spain, 237.

Han Dynasty (206 B.C.–220 A.D.)
> Confucian orthodoxy, scholarship. Disintegration.

Caesar in Gaul, 58 B.C. Dispersion of the Jews, 70 A.D.

The Three Kingdoms (220–280)
> Gains by Buddhism and Taoism. Transitory restoration.

Western Tsin Dynasty (265–316)
> Barbarian invasions.

Plotinus, 205–270. Buddhism in Vietnam. Manicheism in Persia.

North	South	
Barbarian dynasties (350–581)	Six national dynasties (225–589)	Alaric besieges Rome, 408. St. Augustine, 430. Attila, 452.
Wei art, *zen*, Amida.		

THE SECOND EMPIRE

Suei Dynasty (581–617)

Ts'ang Dynasty (618–907)
> Fragmentation.

The Five Dynasties (907–959)
> Limited restoration.

Northern Sung Dynasty (960–1126)
> Neo-Confucianism. Barbarian invasions.

Mahomet in Mecca, 630. Khazori converted to Judaism, 641. Coronation of Charlemagne, Harun al-Rashid, c. 800. First Crusade, 1095.

North	South	
Barbarian dynasties of Leaos and Mongols (907–1125); Kins and Manchus (1115–1234).	Southern Sung Dynasty (1127–1278); Neo-Confucianism. Encyclopedias.	End of the Crusades, 1270. Stabilization of medieval civilization in France in twelfth and thirteenth centuries.

THE THIRD EMPIRE

Mongol Dynasty of the Yuens (1260–1367)
> Religious eclecticism. Theater.

Ming Dynasty (1368–1644)
> Wang Yang-ming, the School of the Heart, criticism of the texts, novels, encyclopedias, the Jesuits.

Beginning of the Hundred Years' War, 1337. Tamerlane in Russia and India, 1398. Islam leaves Spain, fourteenth and fifteenth centuries. Turks enter Constantinople, 1453. Birth of Luther, 1483. Death of Calvin, 1564. Conversion of Henri IV, 1593. The Dutch in Sumatra and Borneo, 1598.

Manchu Dynasty of the Ts'ings (1644–1911).

206

Criticism of the texts. Critical spirit. Encyclopedias. European intervention.

Scientific, industrial, and social revolution. Napoleon.

Republic (1912–1949)

Maritime influences.

New Government (1949–   ).

Hydrogen bomb.

Mainland influences.

As its heading indicates, this bibliographical sketch deals only with the most important, the best known, and the most recent works that I have found useful and even necessary to an understanding of China and Confucius. It amounts to no more than an introduction, though from several points of view. I have given preference to books in French or translated into French whenever I have been able to find them, consult them, or verify their titles. This omits well-known works whose exact titles have slipped my memory.

TEXTS

COUVREUR, S., *Les Quatres livres: III, Entretiens de Confucius et de ses disciples*, Ho-Kien Fu, 1895; later Paris: Cathasia series (Les Belles Lettres).

SSEU-MA TS'IEN, *Mémoires historiques*, 5 volumes, Paris: French translation, Éditions Chavannes, 1905.

The classics, comprising five *kings* and four *shus*, can be found in the Cathasia series in Couvreur's French translations and in two collections, *The Chinese Classics* and *Sacred Books of the East*, in James Legge's English translations. The list of translators of Confucius should include the names of William Soothill, Arthur Waley, Richard Wilhelm, and even Ezra Pound.

BOOKS ON CONFUCIUS

CREEL, H. G., *Confucius, the Man and the Myth*, London: 1951.

ÉTIEMBLE, RENÉ, *Confucius*, Paris: 1956.

EUL-SU YUN, L., *Confucius, sa vie, son oeuvre*, Paris: Maisonneuve, 1942.

GILES, HERBERT, *Confucius and His Rivals*, London: 1915.

GRIPEKOVEN, JEANNE, *Confucius et son temps*, Brussels: 1955.

LIU WU-CHI, *Confucius, His Life and Time*, New York: 1955.

RYGALOFF, ALEXIS, *Confucius*, Paris: 1946.

SHIGEKI KAIZUKA, *Confucius*, New York and London: 1956.

TRAN TRONG-KIM, *Nho-giao (The Doctrine of the Scholars)*, 4 volumes, Hanoi: c. 1923–44; third and fourth editions, 2 volumes, Saigon: Tân Viêt.

WILHELM, RICHARD, *Kungtse, Leben und Lehren*, Leipzig: 1925; Stuttgart: 1950.

GENERAL WORKS

BERNARD-MAITRE, H., *Sagesse chinoise et philosophie chrétienne*, Sienhsien: 1936; Paris (Les Belles Lettres).

CREEL, H. G., *The Birth of China* (in the French translation by Clerc Salles, *la Naissance de la Chine*, preface by Carl W. Bishop), Paris: Payot, 1937.

——, *Chinese Thought From Confucius to Mao Tse-tung*, London: Eyre & Spottiswoode, 1954.

DAO DUY-ANH, *Trung-hoa su-cuong* (*Summary of Chinese History*), new edition, Saigon: Xuât ban Bôn Phuong, 1941.

FONG YEU-LAN, *Précis d'histoire de la philosophie chinoise* (French translation by Guillaume Dunstheimer, preface by P. Demiéville), Paris: Payot, 1952.

GOODRICH, L. CARRINGTON, *A Short History of the Chinese People*, London: Allen & Unwin, 1948.

GRANET, MARCEL, *la Religion des Chinois*, Paris: 1922.

DE GROOT, J. J. M., *The Religious System of China*, 6 volumes, Leyden: 1892, 1912.

HUGHES, E. R., *Chinese Thought in Classical Times*, London and New York: 1942.

KALTENMARK-GHEQUIER, O., *la Littérature chinoise*, Paris: P.U.F., 1948.

KARLGREN, BERNHARD, *Philology and Ancient China*, Oslo and Cambridge: 1926.

LEGGE, JAMES, *The Religions of China*, London: 1880; New York: 1881.

MASPÉRO, HENRI, *la Chine antique*, Paris: 1927, 1955.

——, *les Religions chinoises*, Paris: Musée Guimet, 1950.

HU SHI, *Chong-kuo chö-hio she ta-kang* (*Summary of the History of Chinese Philosophy*), Shanghai: 1919.

——, *The Development of the Logical Method in Ancient China*, Shanghai: 1922.

SUZUKI, D. T., *A Brief History of Early Chinese Philosophy*, London: Probsthain, 1914.

WALEY, ARTHUR, *The Way and Its Power*, London: 1934; later, UNESCO Collection of Representative Works (V, Introduction).

WEBER, MAX, *Konfuzianismus und Taoismus*, in *Gesammelte Aufsätze zur Religionssoziologie*, Berlin: 1920; English translation by Hans H. Gerth, *The Religions of China: Confucianism and Taoism*, Glencoe, Ill.: 1951.

WILHELM, RICHARD, *Histoire de la Civilisation chinoise*, Paris: Payot.

ACKNOWLEDGMENTS

The publishers wish to express their thanks to the curators and staff of the Musée Guimet and the Musée Cernuschi for their assistance in research.

The photographs (by Editions du Seuil) on pages 11, 54, 98, 101, 113, 117, 130, 131, 172, and 176 were taken in the Musée Guimet.

The prints on pages 16 and 87, illustrating scenes in the life of Confucius, as well as the portraits on pages 91, 143, 155, 186, and 187, are taken from *Portraits et éloges de Confucius et des Sages,* a seventeenth-century work (photographs by Editions du Seuil).

The sources for the other illustrations are:

Oswald Siren, *Later China Painting,* page 51 (Musée Guimet), and *Chinese Painting,* pages 111 (Fogg Museum, Cambridge, Mass.), 149 (Huia-hua Kuan, Peking), and 182 (Aba Collection, Osaka Museum).

Corpus des Pierres sculptées Han in the Sinological Center, Peking (University of Paris), pages 41, 42, 162, and 163.

René Grousset, *La Chine et son art,* Plon, pages 12 and 112.

Jack Finegan, *The Archeology of World Religions,* Princeton University Press, page 5.

L. Carrigton Goodrich, *A Short History of the Chinese People,* Allen & Unwin, page 183 (from the Loo Collection, New York).

Chavannes, *Mission Archéologique,* a publication of the Fresc Far-East School, Editions Leroux, 1913, pages 2, 9, 45, 67, 71, 74, 77, 82, 94, 96, 100, 121, 134, 162, 163, 165, and 204.

Chosen Koseki, *Peinture chinoise,* page 104.

Ernest Boerschmann, *La Chine pittoresque (China in Pictures),* Decorative Arts Bookshop, pages 19 and 201.

The Si Yu Ki, Editions du Seuil, page 195.

Photographs: page 3, Agnès Varda; page 126, Chris Marker; pages 4, 13, 108, and 199, Archives Photographiques; pages 59 and 150, Giraudon; page 179, Editions Euros.

The illustrations on pages 9, 41, 42, 45, 59, 67, 74, 77, 82, 96, 100, 162, 163, and 165 are reproductions of prints of Chinese reliefs dating in general from the Han period.

The Chinese characters on pages vi, 25, and 138 were drawn by Lientseng Wang.

INDEX

Abhidarkosa, 185
Agriculturists, School of the, 136, 157
Amitabha, 177
An-she-kao, 174
Anyang, Dynasty of, 10, 12, 13
Aristotle, 114
Asoka, 173
Augustine, St., 118, 182
Avalokiteshvara, 177
Avatamsaka, 185
Avenol, Louis, 196

Bacon, Roger, 122, 190
Baruzi, Joseph, 142
Beyle, 198
Bible, 106, 107, 112, 120; *see also* Catholicism *and* Christianity
Bodhidharma, 177
Book of Lord Shang, The, 145
Brahma-atma, 186
Buck, Pearl, 194
Buddha and Buddhism, 17, 118, 129, 140, 165, 167, 173–178, 183–190, 202, 203; *see also* Zen

Carter, Thomas F., 185
Cathari, heresy of the, 183
Catholicism, 102, 103, 125, 192
Chan kuo (Fighting Kingdoms), 14, 151
Chan kuo ts'ö, 148
Chang (Yin) Dynasty, 10–13, 19, 20, 21, 25, 40, 77, 87, 138, 178
Ch'ang Hong, 43
Chang Tsai, 187, 188, 189
Ch'ang Ts'in, 79
Chang Yi, 148
Chao, Duke of Lu, 29, 48, 49, 56
Chao Kien-tse, 75
Chao-po, 50

Chavannes, 44
Che, 104, 109
Ch'en T'uan, 186
Ch'eng, King of Wei, 40, 43
Cheng (sanctity), 102, 107, 114
Ch'eng (sincerity), 109, 110
Ch'eng Hao, 188, 189
Cheng Ho, 196
Ch'eng Kao-fu, 21, 37
Ch'engs, 52, 53
Cheng-tsai, 22, 23, 24, 33
Ch'eng Yi, 188, 189
Che-Y, 178
Cheyu-sin, 77
Chine Antique, La (Maspéro), 29, 59
Chö, Duke, 82
Chong ("mean"), 116, 118, 119, 120n, 128, 141, 154, 188
Chong-Kong, 106
Chong Yong, 1, 30, 99, 104, 109, 110, 114, 116, 119, 120, 124, 127, 155, 188
Christianity, 104, 109, 127, 182, 190; *see also* Bible *and* Catholicism
Chuan, 2
Chuan-hiu, 8
Chuang, Duke, 53
Chuang-tse, 44, 89, 130, 139, 142, 148
Chu Dynasty, 10–14, 18, 19, 36, 39, 40, 42, 43, 49, 53, 57, 60, 120n, 127, 142
Ch'uen Ts'yu (Spring and Autumn), 1, 2, 14, 31, 58, 84, 85, 96, 151, 153, 166
Chu Hi, 155, 188, 189, 190, 193, 194, 198
Chu-ko Leang, 194
Chu Li, 1

211